D1627035

RELENTLESS

THE SCIENCE OF
BARRIER-BUSTING SALES

SUZANNE C. DUDLEY and TRELITHA R. BRYANT

Edited by Terry Donia

BEHAVIORAL
SCIENCES
RESEARCH
PRESS

Published by Behavioral Sciences Research Press, Inc.
Dallas, Texas

Call Reluctance is a registered trademark of
Behavioral Sciences Research Press, Inc.

Library of Congress Control Number: 2019915173

ISBN 978-0-935907-02-5
Ebook ISBN 978-0-935907-09-4

Some names and identifying details of individuals and organizations described in this book have been changed to protect their privacy.

Due to individual differences and differences of circumstance and setting, the authors and publishers assume no responsibility for the effectiveness of the procedures in this book; and do not intend, state, or imply that this book, or any procedure contained in it, is a substitute for competent medical or mental health intervention when it is required.

First Edition

Book layout and cover design by Bookwise Design
Cover source image by Connect World, Shutterstock.com

CONTENTS

I prayed to the Lord, and he answered me.
He freed me from all my fears.

— PSALM 34:4

ACKNOWLEDGEMENTS

For us, writing a book required a lot of hard work by a lot of people. To adequately thank them all would result in doubling the size of this book, but we will attempt to keep it manageable.

Our names would not be on this book without the extraordinary work of George W. Dudley and Shannon L. Goodson, the pioneers of Call Reluctance research and co-founders of Behavioral Sciences Research Press, Inc. They started our business with $100 and a ground-breaking discovery (during a recession!) and we're still at it 40 years later. They self-published well before it was easy, and they became highly sought-after experts on the topics in this book. Their support for us has been unwavering. We are blessed to pick up the baton, and can only hope to be able to fill their shoes.

Terry Donia, Editorial Goddess, is a miracle worker. If you enjoy reading this book, it's thanks to her. We are constantly amazed by her gifted writing and we are honored to call her our editor. She agreed to work on this project in spite of having a "real job." We couldn't be more grateful . . . and relieved!

Our team at BSRP in Dallas, Texas, is small, but mighty! This book has been a labor of number crunching, digital coordination, researching, logistical planning, and writing. They pitched in, worked extra hours, and pulled it all together without complaint. Thanks to them, it's actually finished and available for purchase. We think they're glad it's over. We haven't told them about the next book yet . . .

Our growing network of Licensed Professional Associates all over the world have provided us with amazing stories of the transformation of salespeople they have helped, and with feedback about how we can better serve salespeople in the future. Thanks to them tens of thousands of salespeople worldwide have learned to manage their hesitation to prospect for new business. They help us extend our reach well beyond anything we could accomplish on our own. They have been patient and steadfast in supporting us through a transition in leadership and the inevitable shift in culture that results. We are blessed to have them on our team, and we're deeply grateful for their advice and support.

And finally, we would like to thank professional salespeople all over the world. You are a blessing to the people you serve and our biggest inspiration. You help people discover solutions they need to make their lives better. In turn, we hope this book makes your life a little bit better.

PREFACE

I n 1986, behavioral scientists George W. Dudley and Shannon L. Goodson released a slim, unassuming book titled *The Psychology of Call Reluctance: How to Overcome the Fear of Self-Promotion*. Although it was marketed as a self-help book for struggling salespeople, within its pages was actually the beginning of a quiet revolution in defining, predicting, and overcoming obstacles to success in sales and beyond.

Dudley and Goodson had studied the factors leading to success or failure in professional salespeople for years . . . and had come to a somewhat unoriginal conclusion: Selling is a numbers game. The more customers you see, the more you sell. Fortunately, that was just a springboard to the research that would make them among the most respected practitioners of serious sales psychology in the world. What they discovered and presented in their first book was this deceptively simple, two-pronged behavioral premise:

1. Closed sales are directly correlated with the number of contacts salespeople initiate with prospective buyers.

2. Many potentially successful salespeople experience fear that limits their ability to initiate those contacts consistently and comfortably.

1

At that time, Call Reluctance — emotional discomfort with prospecting — wasn't being addressed in most sales training programs. Selection tests, employment interviews, and less formal vehicles like self-help books and workshops were designed primarily around a well-worn model of what "good" salespeople were like: Gregarious, aggressive, articulate, money-motivated. Presumed experts from human resources professionals to motivational speakers focused on sales strategies that exploited those traits. But those strategies were overwhelmingly based on an unspoken assumption: That these archetypical superstars could and would consistently seek out prospective customers to sell to.

Dudley and Goodson found that not to be the case. In fact, through hundreds of studies with thousands of salespeople, they stripped back the archetypes (some would say the stereotypes) to reveal the widespread, toxic effects of fear on otherwise motivated, goal-oriented professionals. They developed accurate tests to diagnose it. And they presented effective countermeasures to enable salespeople to overcome the fears that held them back.

The revolution had begun.

That first slim volume described nine distinct forms of Call Reluctance. Dudley and Goodson's next book, *Earning What You're Worth?* (1992), incorporated three additional types discovered in the course of their ongoing research. It also helped broaden the scope of their work beyond sales, helping people in all walks of life to recognize the importance of *visibility management* and tackle the emotional discomfort that keeps them from promoting themselves and their interests.

Over the years Dudley and Goodson's research begat other books, other career assessment tools. But Call Reluctance remained their primary focus. Today there are 16 recognized types. Sales organizations around the world utilize Call Reluctance applications to hire and train employees who consistently prospect for new customers. Countless careers have been transformed via psychologically sound techniques to overcome self-limiting fears.

So why another book about Call Reluctance now?

The business world is a very different place than it was when Dudley and Goodson began their research. It's more diverse, more internationally-focused, and more willing to adapt and evolve to stay competitive. The landscape of selling has also changed, shaped by technology, global economics, societal norms, and arguably Call Reluctance research itself. The idea that the foundation of success is a culture of prospecting rather than a cult of personality has taken root and flourished in forward-thinking sales organizations everywhere.

At the same time, companies and individuals today are exposed to far more information — about far more topics — than ever before. Anyone with a website can self-identify as an expert. Anyone with an e-book can be a guru. Even for the most laser-focused it can be difficult to filter out trolls, scammers, and other counterproductive noise claiming to be the truth about . . . well, anything. Good advice isn't always good, and common sense is hardly common.

That's why Dudley and Goodson's groundbreaking research remains relevant. Rooted in science, and reliably immune to self-help fads and feel-good hyperbole, the psychology of Call Reluctance has applications that reach far beyond traditional "selling." In today's world we are all, or should be, advocates for our own success. We can all benefit from proudly and ethically promoting ourselves to others.

This book aims to bring decades of research, and results, into the 21st century. It's designed to speak to young adults who weren't even born when *The Psychology of Call Reluctance* was published, as well as to seasoned pros who were prospecting before millennials were a gleam in a marketer's eye. Unlike Dudley and Goodson's previous books, it presents Call Reluctance research as the settled science it is. If you're new to the visibility management party, a wealth of research-based evidence is still available in those seminal works, as well as in the workshops we present all over the world. If you've followed Dudley and Goodson for a while, this book streamlines and updates their work in what we hope is a fresh, focused format for the modern professional.

Are you ready to be relentless in your pursuit of sales success? Turn the page and let's begin. We hope you enjoy it as much as we've enjoyed bringing it to you.

1

Hi, My Name Is _____

A re you in sales?

For some reading this, the answer is unequivocal: "Yes — I sell (insurance, computers, financial services) for a living. That's what it says on my business card, that's what I do."

For others, the answer is less straightforward: "Well, I take a more consultative approach to my business. I consider myself more a relationship manager than a common salesperson."

And some folks are already rolling their eyes and wondering where this is heading: "Look. I'm no salesperson. I just want to see if I can get anything useful out of this book. I'll give you about three pages to get to the bottom line, or I'm out of here."

Still others will give different answers. You get the idea. So let's cut to the chase. Are you in sales? The answer is YES.

For a long time — years, even generations — there was a widely accepted definition of a professional salesperson: Someone (but typically a man) who lived by selling things. Tangible things, like cars, or less tangible things, like insurance policies. The product didn't matter. The customer didn't matter. To the salesperson, only closing the sale mattered, and by any means necessary.

As a result, salespeople possessed (we won't say enjoyed) a well-defined reputation in society. They were presumed to be outgoing, fearless, audacious. Money-motivated, competitive, ruthless. Moored to ethical standards with the loosest of ropes, they would say and do whatever it took to close the deal.

Those presumptions were reflected, and amplified, in popular culture. In 1949's *Death of a Salesman*, playwright Arthur Miller created "Willy Loman," the iconic self-centered, insecure peddler who became the fictional gold standard of the stereotypical salesman. In the 1980s, David Mamet doubled down on hyper-aggressive sales stereotypes in *Glengarry Glen Ross*, portraying a foul-mouthed boys' club driven to succeed in real estate through a combination of greed and desperation. And along the way were all manner of door-to-door salesmen and shady used-car dealers played for laughs and ridiculed in movies, TV, and cartoons.

Aren't you glad you're in sales?

But wait. Fortunately, times have changed. For one thing, selling is no longer a "man's game." Many women enjoy successful sales careers, changing the face of the global sales force forever. The perceived legitimacy of the profession has also evolved, with respected universities like

Baylor and Ball State offering undergraduate degrees in sales (and many more being added each year). And selling itself has changed. In an effort to dispel old stereotypes, many industries have shifted to a non-traditional sales model that's less transactional and one-sided, more "client-focused," "need-based," or "solution-centered." At least that's the way training companies pitch their programs to sales-based businesses, and the way those businesses in turn position themselves to customers. Whether it's actually true is up for debate. More on that later.

Despite changes in approach and demographics, the image of salespeople and the sales profession in the collective imagination has remained surprisingly stable. A 2013 study compared editorial cartoons featuring salespeople that were published before 2000 to those published since 2000 (that year was chosen because it approximates the introduction of widely used sales management software, as well as the rise of modern "consultative" approaches to selling). The comparison revealed that over the years little has changed when it comes to the frequency of jokes made about salespeople and overall (negative) popular attitudes toward them, even though the profession itself changed significantly.[1] The "sales game" was and is seen by many as primarily pushing products, chasing quotas, and earning flashy status symbols like pink Cadillacs and Rolex watches. Those are the things salespeople (supposedly) care about and build their careers around.

But how much of that pervasive persona is grounded in reality? How much is simply the tattered remnants of outdated stereotypes that stubbornly refuse to die? How much do you unwittingly accept those stereotypes as you navigate your own career?

Think of how you answered the question we posed at the start of this chapter. Were you able to easily accept a sales-oriented identity (regardless of what you were educated or trained to do for a living)? Did you willingly adopt an alternative, "softer" description of how you conduct yourself in business? Or did you reject outright the notion that you, in fact, "sell" something every single day?

If you resisted or dismissed the idea that you're in sales, right now, we respectfully disagree. This is the 21st century. *Everyone* is in sales. Everyone has an idea to promote, a talent to offer, a service to provide to, or on behalf of, others. Something, or someone, to advocate for. You do, too, even if you haven't (yet) thought of it in terms of "selling."

Don't believe us? Complete this sentence:

"My primary professional goal over the next 12 months is to _____." Thinking about how you filled in the blank, take a few minutes to answer these questions:

1. What do I need to do to accomplish that goal?

2. Who could help me do it?

3. How do I let them know I need their help?

4. If I don't already personally know the individual(s) I need to talk to, how do I connect with them?

Whatever your personal or professional goals may be, chances are at some point you'll need other people to help bring them to fruition. People who will buy from you, believe in you, invest in you, make introductions for you. They can only do it if they know what you need. They can only do *that* if they know who you are. And the most effective way to make sure they do is to seek them out and tell them yourself, as often and as persuasively as necessary.

ADVOCACY AND THE FOUR I'S

If you want to achieve what's most important to you, it's vital to be your own best advocate. *Advocacy* is intentional, outcome-oriented promotion of an idea, a position, a decision. It's moving closer to a goal by bringing other people closer to it through your actions. Selling is a type of advocacy; so are job-seeking, campaigning, promoting, and fundraising. There are tactical differences between, say, selling stocks and positioning yourself for a promotion or seeking backers for a new business. But regardless of the *environment*, successful advocacy relies on the same *process*. Let's break it down.

The advocacy process consists of four functional dimensions. They describe the behaviors consistently employed by successful advocates everywhere. We call them the **Four I's**.

Initiate: This is when you identify and make contact with prospective clients (customers, employers, decision-makers, etc.). It might happen in a formal presentation, an informal chat, a phone call, a speech, or any other type of initial communication.

Introduce: This is how you let prospective clients know who you are and what you offer. It's typically the first information you provide after you've initiated contact.

Inform: This is when you share information about your product or service and, just as important, get your prospects to share what they want or need from you.

Influence: This is the active, persuasive role you take in the prospect's buying decision; it's how you get to the closed sale.

The advocacy process encompasses all the things you do to advance your interests, whether they be professional goals, like career success, or personal milestones, such as contributing meaningfully to society. It allows you to define and pursue what you want out of life. We think it's a life discipline everyone should be comfortable embracing.

Being an effective advocate doesn't require you to assume a persona or alter your values. You don't have to be "Ricky Roma" from *Glengarry Glen Ross* if that's not who you are. But it does require you to manage your visibility in the marketplace, whatever that market may be.

In the chapters ahead, you're going to learn how to

apply the Four I's to your career. We hope you find the information engaging, relevant, and entertaining. We know it's effective, because it's based on the pioneering work of respected psychologists George W. Dudley and Shannon L. Goodson. Their research is the gold standard for helping professional salespeople comfortably and consistently prospect for new business. We're proud to continue and expand their legacy of scientific study.

As you read, you'll encounter terminology that reflects the original focus of Dudley and Goodson's research on professional salespeople. Terms like "selling," "prospecting," "cold calling," and "sales quotas" will be very familiar to some readers. If you're in professional sales, that language is part of your everyday vocabulary. But other readers work in environments where traditional sales jargon may not directly apply to their typical objectives and activities. If that describes you, don't feel left out. You're definitely invited to this party. Consider how terms like "selling" and "prospecting" apply to you within the broader context of advocacy. For example:

➡️ **Job seekers:** In order to land a desirable position within a reasonable timeframe, it's critical that you:
  - Initiate contact with ALL the people in your social and professional network.
  - Initiate contact with professional organizations in your area of expertise (for instance, you can dramatically increase your visibility in the job market by offering to give a timely and relevant presentation to a group of your peers).

- Attend events hosted by your industry association to initiate contact with people you don't know (otherwise known as networking).

  All of these things make your competence *visible* so that it can be *recognized* so that the right person can *reward* you with a job.

➡ **Relationship builders:** All of the above "prospecting" activities for job seekers apply to relationship builders, too. One university professor we met told us that "prospecting" is for "transactional sellers" and not relevant for "professional salespeople who build relationships." But you can't build a relationship with someone who doesn't know you exist. What's more, continually building new relationships will help inoculate your career against the natural fluctuations that are inherent in any business.

➡ **Academics:** While some PhDs probably believe they'll eventually get tenure simply because they exist (and are probably still bitterly waiting), the truth is very different. The people who make tenure decisions need to know you and be familiar with your accomplishments. Who better to tell them than you? The same goes for securing grant money. Would you have a better chance of getting the funds you want if you were highly visible within your area of expertise? How do you make that happen?

➡ **Job promotion candidates:** You have to sell
yourself to the decision-makers in your organization. Are you waiting for someone to decide
that you're so fantastic they'll simply call you in
and offer you more money? (Spoiler alert: Your
immediate superior is probably more worried
about his own promotion than yours.) Who, beyond your immediate supervisor, needs to know
who you are and what you do well to get on your
company's advancement radar? Your version of
"prospecting" in this case is initiating contact or
attending networking events to ensure that the
right people in your organization know about
you and your skills. Talk to enough people, and
even if your company doesn't come through for
you, another one probably will.

➡ **Entrepreneurs:** The importance of advocacy
here should be self-evident, but again and again
we find it not to be the case. Breaking news:
You'll never land any clients who don't know
you exist. You have to be *visible* to grab and grow
market share . . . and that means prospecting for
new business. Constantly.

➡ **Professional services (CPAs, attorneys, engi-
neers, etc.):** Want to be a partner in your firm?
Do you think you get there with mad technical skills alone? No. You get there by having a
positive impact on the bottom line. That means
identifying potential new clients and bringing

them on board. That's what good salespeople do. Ask them how. They can help!

➡ **Doctors, dentists, other medical professionals:** Due to insurance laws and other changes, your practice is probably more complicated and messy than ever before. There's a lot you can't control — but there's a lot you can, as well. Do you want to attract more of a certain demographic in your patient base — say, young families or people with greater disposable income? How many potential new patients do you think you could find if you went looking for them by giving presentations to organizations that represented their interests (like the PTA or civic organizations)? That's prospecting!

There are so many ways the Four I's can help you move closer to your goals, no matter what they are. So, for the rest of this book, rest assured that when we say "prospecting" and "selling," we're talking to you!

ETHICAL VS. UNETHICAL SELF-PROMOTION

Many people — both inside and outside professional sales — believe that advocacy by any other name amounts to nothing more than self-promotion, and that self-promotion is inherently undesirable behavior for various reasons. Some equate it with showing off, or hogging the spotlight, or taking advantage of others. They may have been raised with these beliefs or acquired them as the result of negative experiences with shameless, unethical self-promoters. They're reluctant to advocate their own interests because they don't want others to see them the same way.

The truth is, there's nothing congenitally unseemly about self-promotion, whether it's done to sell a product, find a job, or build a business. Some people do it naturally. Some are downright gifted at shining a spotlight on themselves. People like Lebron James, Martha Stewart, and the Kardashians are natural self-promoters. They instinctively find ways to make themselves visible, to advance themselves and their "brand." They are consistently, as Theodore Roosevelt put it, "in the arena." They may or may not be the best at what they do in life. But they reap the rewards as if they were. You don't have to like them, or admire them, but you can't deny their ability to successfully manage their visibility.

Like any other career-supportive behavior, self-promotion can be undertaken ethically and with respect for others, or it can be practiced to use and exploit people. The choice is yours.

Over the years we've seen countless examples of both types of self-promotion. We've developed a checklist to help you spot unethical self-promoters — to help prevent being taken advantage of by them, and to help you keep from joining their ranks as you promote yourself.

HOW TO SPOT UNETHICAL SELF-PROMOTERS

- They're compulsive name-droppers — they know absolutely everyone you need them to know to impress you with their social standing and connections.
- They claim *expertise,* not just familiarity, in an unrealistic number of fields and won't simply admit when they don't know something.
- They have many short-term, superficial business connections, but few deep and long-lasting relationships.
- Their primary tools for influencing others are charm and endearment rather than competence and experience.
- They maintain an inappropriate level of calm and composure, even when caught in a lie.
- When confronted with evidence of deception, they dismiss their dishonesty as "a harmless misunderstanding."
- Their boasts of past successes conceal a history of legal entanglements and previous "misunderstandings."
- They pretend to share your values, interests, and objectives in an effort to sway your opinions, but their actions don't actually reflect them.
- They traffic in the language of sincerity — using words like "honesty," "integrity," and "values" — without displaying it in their behavior.
- They project their ethical shortcomings onto others, saying things like "everybody does it" and "you'd do the same thing if you were in my shoes."

We're not saying that engaging in one or two of these behaviors, or occasionally adopting them, makes someone an unethical self-promoter. But if you find yourself dealing with a person who displays a consistent pattern of the above behavioral markers, you may be dealing with an ethically compromised individual. Our best advice would be to keep one hand on your wallet and back away.

The best way to avoid falling into the murky trap of unethical self-promotion yourself is to continually gauge your actions against known standards of ethical behavior. We've developed a handy yardstick you can apply to your self-promotional efforts to see if they measure up. It consists of the following benchmarks called the **Four C's**.

Candor: Is your behavior forthright and honest? Do you tell the truth without hesitation or reservation (even when it would be easy not to do so)?

Correspondence: Do you represent yourself and your product faithfully? Can the claims you make be verified against known facts?

Completeness: Do you give people comprehensive information without withholding "inconvenient" or harmful data in an attempt to deceive them? (Note: Successful salespeople often hold certain details in reserve for strategic reasons. The *intent to deceive* is the important metric here.)

Consistency: Is your representation of the facts the same today as it was yesterday? Can you be counted on to speak without deviation or contradiction?

Some behaviors are objectively shameful. Taking candy from a baby. Kicking a puppy. Casually giving away the end of a movie without dropping a ***SPOILER ALERT***. But prospecting and self-promotion? Why would you be ashamed of advocating for a product, service, goal, or cause you believe in, and doing so with pride and purpose?

In a rational world this would never happen. But the world isn't always rational, and the least rational place in it can be your own mind. It can be hard to overcome years of feeling emotionally uncomfortable with the idea of blowing your own horn. We understand. We're not natural self-promoters ourselves. But in our own careers we've learned to embrace advocacy in order to move closer to goals that are important to us, and we've been able to reap the financial rewards of doing so. If it can work for us, it can work for anybody.

2

Sales Call Reluctance:
The Advocacy Gap in Action

Achieving personal or professional success requires you to advocate for your interests. Selling, in the traditional sense of convincing people to buy a product or service, is a subset of advocacy. They share fundamental behaviors, although the terminology may vary. The only differences between traditional salespeople and successful advocates in any other walk of life are superficial. The titles. The platforms. The stereotypes.

In our research, we've historically chosen to focus on advocacy as it relates to professional sales. In doing so, we swim in a crowded pool. Training and self-help programs created specifically for salespeople aren't difficult to find. Actually, they're hard to avoid (and if their creators are successfully practicing what they preach, they should be). Competing books, seminars, websites, even YouTube videos clamor for attention and promise to turn you into a selling machine with a license to print money. A quick search of Amazon's best-selling books on the subject (as of late 2018) reveals the hottest themes currently enticing would-be sales superstars to invest their time and money in self-improvement:

- Overcoming Objections
- Building Client Relationships
- Applying "Positive Psychology"
- Using Technology/Artificial Intelligence
- "Neuromarketing"
- "Values-Based" Customer Service
- Asking Power Questions
- Creating Urgency
- Solution Selling
- Performance Analytics
- Closing Strategies

And that's just scratching the surface of what's available. We don't intend to compile a comprehensive list. Moreover, we prefer to remain neutral when it comes to the effectiveness of any of these approaches. Our position is that, when applied thoughtfully and diligently, they can all be useful tools. Only you can decide if they're worth your attention.

For our purposes, in evaluating these and other self-help and training applications that promote their ability to transform your productivity, we note that many suffer from one (or both) of two essential flaws. While they may have their merits, embedded within their philosophies and advice are dangerous assumptions that, accepted uncritically, can render them ineffective and even dangerous to your sales career.

The first assumption has to do with the supposed adversarial nature of sales. According to the old stereotypes, the very idea of "selling" to people involves conflict, a hurdle you must clear at the beginning and end of every sale, and at every step in between. As a baseline for sales training, the idea has its roots in the 1960s, when Xerox developed a program called Professional Selling Skills (PSS) for its sales force. PSS defined success as " . . . abandoning high-pressure sales tactics and adopting a more consultative approach to selling . . . to build customer trust and rapport . . . " This framework caught on worldwide with sales organizations that were eager to find a new "hook" to motivate salespeople and buyers alike. It opened the floodgates to the "soft-sell" movement, which reached its peak around the turn of the 21st century. Everywhere you looked, common salespeople were transformed into "consultants" — needs-based, customer-focused solutions partners — armed with buzzwords and eager to please. Like so many ugly ducklings, they positioned themselves as beautiful, rapport-building swans to woo prospective clients.

Unfortunately, in some environments soft-selling eventually turned rigid. Relentless corporate emphasis on customer rapport and "consultative" selling devolved into a pedantic, inflexible refrain: Relationships good, selling bad. It wasn't enough to give salespeople additional tools and training to supplement their efforts. Taken to extremes by short-sighted organizations, the "soft" approach resulted in a complete makeover of word, thought, and deed. In an effort to comply with the "rules" of this type of selling, sales organizations of all types began to strip away core components of traditional selling styles. Commission structures were scrapped, because they "encouraged greed." Business cards were redesigned to replace the unseemly position of "salesperson" with trendy, warm-and-fuzzy titles like "relationship manager," "adviser," and "customer care specialist." Closing questions designed to persuade were discouraged in favor of gentle "dialogues" that (supposedly) allowed customers to experience a purchasing epiphany in a pressure-free vacuum.

Ironically, these same organizations unwittingly set their "client managers" up for failure. While radically shaping *how* products and services were sold, they continued to reward sellers for the same thing they always had: results. The last time we checked, companies weren't paying relationship bonuses or rapport incentives. They overwhelmingly were and are measuring success based on closed sales, period. Like a faulty GPS, they were recalculating their salespeople's route toward a convoluted detour while still expecting them to reach their destination on time.

We dispute the implied (and sometimes explicitly stated) message that ethical selling behavior requires a drastic makeover to make it more palatable to customers. Selling isn't inherently a bad thing, and people who choose to make their living in sales shouldn't have to pretend to be something else to thrive. Sales as a profession is no different from any other. You can and should take pride in doing it well. And you can and should strive to be an ethical practitioner. But simply having "salesperson" on your business card isn't a judgment on your character, just as having "consultant" there isn't proof that you travel on a higher moral plane. Building rapport with customers is a valuable skill, but it's not the ultimate goal. Closing sales is. Be skeptical of anyone who attempts to convince you otherwise.

The second flawed assumption we see in many sales training applications isn't a matter of content, but of timing. Sales is a competitive business. Any skill or technique that gives an edge over the competition (ethically, of course) has value. Their effectiveness for you personally will vary depending on your product, your clients, your selling environment, and many other factors. But many of the tips, tricks, and strategies on offer tend to have one thing in common: They come into play when you're in front of prospective customers. In other words, they only make a difference *after* you've initiated contact with buyers. And they assume that you already do that on a consistent basis. We've found that to be a fatal flaw in many otherwise valuable programs.

Here's why. Selling is a numbers game. Figures vary by industry, but generally speaking, it takes about 25 contacts to net 12 responses, which result in five sales presentations and three closed sales. Those interactions correspond to the Four I's of advocacy: Initiate, introduce, inform, and influence. It's fairly simple, then, for anyone to calculate the number of contacts they need to make on a daily or weekly basis to meet their goals, and then go out and make them.

But the Four I's, while all critical to success, have to

occur in order. You can't rearrange them, and you can't leave any out. Which means that, regardless of price, personality, or presentation, the sales process is stuck in neutral unless and until you get in front of potential new customers. Initiating contact isn't necessarily the most important step in selling. But it has to come *first*.

For salespeople who resemble the old stereotypes — fearless, aggressive, all the well-known tropes — consistently putting themselves in front of prospective buyers is second nature. They do it with ease. But most don't. For them, the numbers don't add up because they can't, don't, or won't initiate contact in sufficient numbers to support their goals.

Years of research have shown that behind the media-fueled stereotypes, many salespeople secretly struggle with a bone-shaking fear of prospecting. They're dogged by persistent negative thoughts of what might happen when they pick up the phone or step into a prospect's office. No matter what they sell, how well they've been trained, how good they are at time management and goal-setting, and/or how much they believe in their product or service, their discomfort can cut off opportunities for new business by making prospecting emotionally difficult. They don't get a chance to use their selling skills because they don't see as many prospects, as often, or as consistently as they could or should.

It's called Call Reluctance, and it belies the pop-culture image of salespeople as a tribe of glad-handing extroverts. A whopping 85 percent of professional salespeople experience it to some degree. The consequences can be devastating: Studies show that up to 80 percent of all salespeople who fail in their first year do so because of insufficient prospecting. Even among sales veterans, Call Reluctance exacts a toll — 40 percent report experiencing one or more episodes of Call Reluctance that has made them consider leaving sales, regardless of their years of experience or current income level.

If you're not in traditional sales, you may find it helpful to refer to Call Reluctance as the Fear of Self-Promotion or The Advocacy Gap. To us, the label isn't important. By any name your fears, left unchecked, will place an artificial cap on the number of contacts you're able to initiate, reducing your visibility and limiting what you can accomplish. According to George W. Dudley, the dean of Call Reluctance research, American salespeople overall could be closing as much as 40–60 percent more sales, directly affecting the American economy, if they were more comfortable with prospecting, networking, and other types of contact initiation. Do the math. What would that improvement mean to your bottom line?

Despite being so widespread (and so costly), many people suffer in silence with sales Call Reluctance. They assume they're simply "too shy" to successfully promote themselves and therefore undeserving of the rewards enjoyed by those who are less impaired. Accepting their emotional hesitation as a character flaw or an immutable personality trait, they fail to recognize their discomfort as an artificial barrier, a framework of behaviors that was systematically constructed and can be just as deliberately dismantled. Instead, many settle for far less than they could achieve if they were able to comfortably and consistently initiate contacts with prospective customers.

But it doesn't have to be that way. Fortunately, help is available. We've been assessing sales Call Reluctance and providing effective solutions for more than 40 years. Today, sales organizations all over the world have benefited from authentic Call Reluctance research and applications.

Results-oriented managers and trainers realize that it's not enough to have a great product, and it's not enough to have highly trained staff who know how to sell it. It's not enough to give salespeople the latest technology to track their customers, or multimedia presentations embedded with the most persuasive bells and whistles. Those things are important. But they assume that salespeople are already initiating contact with potential buyers. Salespeople with Call Reluctance aren't, or not at levels that support their personal and organizational goals.

Whether your professional goals depend on signed purchase orders, freelance writing assignments, or community support, it's important to understand how fear may be limiting you right now. The next, equally important step is to apply practical countermeasures that can help you become a relentless prospector.

With that in mind, let's start with a self-rating scale to gauge your current attitudes toward prospecting and contact initiation. This is hardly an in-depth diagnostic tool, but it's an effective general indicator of how much your fears may be impairing you. Open a blank document or get out a sheet of paper, and record your answers to the following questions. Remember to think in terms of what "prospecting" means in your professional situation.

CALL RELUCTANCE SELF-RATING SCALE

1. I probably spend more time planning to prospect than I devote to actually prospecting. Yes or No?

2. I'm probably not really trying to prospect for new business as much as I could or should, because I'm not sure it's worth the hassle any more. Yes or No?

3. I probably don't try as often as I could to initiate contact with influential people in my community who might be candidates for my product/service, or at least a source of referrals. Yes or No?

4. I get really uncomfortable when I have to phone someone I don't know, who isn't expecting my call, to persuade them to buy something they may not want. Yes or No?

5. Personally, I think having to call people I don't know, who aren't expecting my call, to promote a product or service is humiliating and demeaning. Yes or No?

6. Self-promotion doesn't really bother me. I just don't apply myself to it very purposefully or consistently. Yes or No?

7. I try to avoid giving group presentations if I can. Yes or No?

8. Actually, prospecting doesn't really bother me. I could initiate more contacts if I didn't have so many other things on my plate competing for my time and energy. Yes or No?

9. I find myself hesitating when it's time to ask for a referral from an existing client. Yes or No?

10. I usually need time to psych myself up before I initiate contact with anyone. Yes or No?

11. I tend to spend a lot of time planning, prioritizing, re-sorting, and categorizing the names on my prospect list before I actually start contacting them. Yes or No?

12. Making cold calls (contacting people I don't know who aren't expecting my call) on a regular basis is really difficult for me. Yes or No?

13. I tend to feel uneasy when I prospect because deep down I think that consistently promoting yourself or your business is not very respectable. Yes or No?

14. To me, making sales presentations to my friends or asking them for referrals is unacceptable because it might look like I'm trying to exploit their friendship. Yes or No?

15. I often worry that I might be intruding on people when I prospect. Yes or No?

16. To me, making sales presentations to members of my own family, or just asking them for referrals, is unacceptable because it might look like I'm trying to exploit them selfishly. Yes or No?

17. It's important to me to find innovative, alternative ways to prospect that are more professional and dignified than the methods other salespeople use. Yes or No?

18. I think that prospecting for new business probably takes more out of me emotionally than it does other people. Yes or No?

19. I'm OK in one-on-one selling situations, but I would probably get really nervous if I found out I had to give a sales presentation in front of a group. Yes or No?

20. Highfalutin people like lawyers and CEOs tend to annoy me, so I don't try to initiate contact with them, even though I probably could if I really wanted to. Yes or No?

21. Self-help material, like this self-rating scale, is superficial and probably won't tell me anything I don't already know. Yes or No?

22. I have reasonably clear goals, but I probably spend more time talking about them than working toward them. Yes or No?

23. I would probably feel more positive about prospecting for new business if I had some additional training. Yes or No?

24. I could probably prospect more, but I'm just marking time until I get to do what I *really* want to do. Yes or No?

Scoring

Determine your overall score by adding up your "yes" responses. Then read the interpretive summary for your score range below.

1–3

Indicates one of two conditions: Either you experience no emotional difficulty whatsoever associated with prospecting, or you actually do experience some stress but you're hesitant or emotionally unable to reveal how much, even to yourself. Either way, keep reading. This book can help you inoculate yourself against Call Reluctance carriers.

4–6

Indicates that you're like most other people who need to promote themselves and their product. The fear of self-promotion is present, but only in low, non-toxic amounts. It may be occasionally annoying, but it's not likely to be serious at this level. It should be manageable by simply emphasizing the markets and prospecting techniques you're most comfortable with and avoiding the ones that feel most threatening. This book can still be helpful, however, because it can strengthen your tender prospecting areas, opening up even more prospecting possibilities down the road.

7–9

You probably experience moderate or intermittent levels of Call Reluctance. One or more forms are currently limiting your prospecting activity to a level beneath your ability. Low prospecting probably keeps you from exploiting the full potential of the opportunities available to you. The techniques in this book should be personally and financially rewarding.

10–12

Your answers suggest a considerable amount of Call Reluctance right now. Your prospecting may be only a shadow of what it could be (or needs to be to reach your goals). Don't despair. Instead, fasten your seat belt and keep reading. In our experience, people who score like you get the most benefit out of the countermeasures described in this book.

13 or more

Oh, wow. According to your score, you could have enough Call Reluctance to stop a small sales force. Are you comfortable making calls on *any* prospective buyers? If your answers are truly indicative of your attitudes toward prospecting and self-promotion, then you should consider taking immediate corrective steps. This book can help you turn your career around, if you let it.

There's one other possible interpretation. You may be too self-critical. In abnormal psych class, did you think every pathology pertained to you? When your pastor talks about sin, do you assume he's accusing you directly? When taking self-assessments like this one, is the most negative response typically your default? If you think you might have been too hard on yourself, take it again. Be honest, but not brutally so. Your condition may be less terminal than you think.

YOUR CALL RELUCTANCE PROFILE

Almost no one is afflicted with all 16 types. Such an extreme diagnosis occurs in less than 0.5 percent of individuals. That almost certainly doesn't include you. (Remember what we said about being too self-critical.) Studies show that most people in sales experience difficulty with up to five forms of prospecting behavior. The 16 types will be covered in detail in later chapters. Chances are you'll recognize yourself in a few of them. That's when you'll want to continue to the chapter about treating Call Reluctance with simple, proven behavioral techniques.

Effective treatment always starts with an accurate diagnosis. Now that you know how predisposed to Call Reluctance you are, let's begin to tease out the specific sources of your discomfort. Once again, the following

"Prospecting EKG" isn't a full-blown assessment, but it can help establish your Call Reluctance profile heading into the in-depth descriptions to come.

Just as you did the with earlier self-rating scale, record your answers to each of the following questions.

1. How many total contacts did you initiate during your last full workweek?

2. Approximately how much time do you spend preparing for each new contact you make?

3. How many group or seminar-style presentations did you give or try to schedule last month?

4. How many presentations or requests for contacts, referrals, or connections did you initiate with your personal friends and acquaintances last month?

5. How many sales-related conversations did you initiate while attending business, civic, social, political, or religious gatherings during the last month?

6. How many appointments, interviews, or other promotional meetings were you persuaded to reschedule during the last month?

7. How many contacts or conversations did you try to initiate last week with high-level professionals or wealthy, influential people in your community?

8. How many sales-related conversations or requests for contacts, referrals, or connections did you initiate during the last month with members of your own family? (Skip this question if members of your family aren't available due to distance, death, or estrangement.)

9. Approximately how many times during the last full workweek did you try to think of new, innovative prospecting methods that wouldn't feel demeaning to you or offensive to prospective clients?

10. Approximately how many times during the last full workweek did you ask people you know (including current clients) for names of other people you could call on (referrals)? How many times *could* you have asked for referrals in that period?

11. Approximately how many phone calls did you attempt to make to prospective buyers during the last full workweek? Approximately how many *could* you have attempted?

12. How many times did you post about your product or service on social media during the last workweek?

13. In the last few weeks, approximately how many initial or follow-up calls did you make to decision-makers within an organization as part of an ongoing effort to negotiate a deal?

14. How many attempts have you made this month to ask an existing customer if they were interested in an upgrade or add-on to a recent sale?

15. How much time do you typically spend building rapport with prospective clients compared with the amount of time spent closing sales and discussing payment?

16. Optional: Describe any circumstances you believe had a significant influence on how you answered any of the above questions. If you wish, include comments about the questions, the relevance of this exercise to your particular situation, or any other observations you wish to make.

ANALYZING YOUR EKG

So . . . Are you normal? What's "normal"? That's a loaded question under any circumstances, but for our purposes the answer is: It depends. Prospecting — consistently managing your visibility as appropriate to meet your goals — varies from profession to profession, from industry to industry, from product to product, and from company to company. That means the "right" kind of prospecting in one setting could be a serious problem in another. If you work in an environment that provides guidance and training from sales managers, trainers, mentors, or helpful peers, share this assessment with them. Start a conversation about whether your answers are high, low, or normal for your situation. Unlike the yes or no responses on the earlier self-assessment scale, the Prospecting EKG requires reflection on the *difference* between your answers and the numbers that are most likely to result in success for *you*. Those gaps represent areas where you're most likely to find opportunities for improvement.

Do you think you could be doing more to prospect and self-promote? Do you think Call Reluctance could be holding you back? Or are there other issues standing between you and the success you're capable of achieving?

There's one way to find out: Keep reading.

3

The Impostors

ales Call Reluctance research conducted by Dudley and Goodson and their associates comprises hundreds of validated, scientific studies of hundreds of thousands of sales professionals across multiple countries. It forms the basis of hiring and training best practices in sales organizations around the world. When it comes to detecting and measuring authentic sales Call Reluctance, they literally wrote the book.

But that hasn't stopped many self-proclaimed sales experts from claiming that they have a "truly different approach" to tackling the problem of sub-par sales performance. Such approaches often focus on improving the overall sales *process:* initiating, introducing, informing, and influencing. But while skill-based sales training is important, it often fails to acknowledge that Call Reluctance primarily affects the critical *first* step in that process: initiating, or prospecting. Training topics like lead-qualifying, product knowledge, and rapport-building, while helpful, neither immunize against Call Reluctance nor treat its underlying causes. Learning to sell, or sell differently, puts the selling cart before the prospecting horse. It's wasted effort if you can't, don't, or won't initiate contact with prospective buyers on a consistent basis.

If you struggle with prospecting fears, don't be swayed by practitioners who lack the knowledge or the empathy to provide meaningful assistance. They may (or may not) be well-intentioned, but their primary focus is on retrofitting a definition of selling that matches what they want to teach you.

Some gurus address Call Reluctance by denying the problem even exists. One author takes this strikingly tone-deaf (and inaccurate) approach: "Call Reluctance is an easy label to apply because it seems to cover all sales sins. If you are . . . so afraid to call that you can't will your fingers to dial the phone or your feet to move . . . quit. Go do something else . . . You don't have Call Reluctance; you are doing something you hate."

Other self-styled experts take the position that Call Reluctance afflicts only the novice salesperson. Their common refrain is that "getting a few successful calls under your belt" is the golden ticket to overcoming prospecting fears. Yet our research shows that this isn't the case. While Call Reluctance scores may show a small decrease among sales veterans (those with 5+ years of tenure), time and experience alone don't immunize most sales professionals against the costly effects of fear (see table).

CALL RELUCTANCE BY EXPERIENCE

Call Reluctance Type	< 5 Years	> 5 Years	"F"	p	Effect Size
Total Call Reluctance	38	31	212.882	.000	0.076
Doomsayer	20	10	111.197	.000	0.041
Over-Preparation	49	41	108.993	.000	0.041
Hyper-Pro	38	32	48.075	.000	0.018
Role Rejection	38	30	136.621	.000	0.050
Yielder	52	42	191.440	.000	0.069
Oppositional Reflex	16	15	2.599	.107	0.001
Stage Fright	47	37	183.853	.000	0.067
Social Self-Consciousness	35	26	136.986	.000	0.051
Friendshield	35	30	49.333	.000	0.019
Famshield	35	31	27.895	.000	0.011
Referral Aversion	36	30	77.893	.000	0.029
Telephobia	38	30	88.812	.000	0.033
Online Prospecting Discomfort	33	28	25.393	.000	0.010
Complex Sales	46	36	132.495	.000	0.049
Sales Extensions	33	25	138.837	.000	0.051
Arranging Payment	49	39	192.835	.000	0.070
Motivation	63	67	18.994	.000	0.007
Goal Level	62	67	50.414	.000	0.019
Goal Diffusion	50	47	7.318	.007	0.003

N = 2574; < 5 Years = 777; > 5 Years = 1797; General Sales; United States

Our approach to Call Reluctance is different. It's based on science, which doesn't lend itself to catchy sound bites or wisecracks, but has the virtue of being measurable and verifiable. It may not be seductive, but it's effective. With that in mind, let's take a look at what Call Reluctance actually is, based on decades of scientific study. Just as important, let's examine what it isn't.

DEFINING THE PROBLEM: PRODUCT AND PROCESS

The most concrete evidence for the existence of Call Reluctance comes directly from its effect on prospecting activity. We use the *product definition* of Call Reluctance to describe the problem in terms of its result, or product: low prospecting activity.

"Prospecting activity" simply means the total number of face-to-face and other direct contacts you initiate with prospective clients. *Genuine Call Reluctance always results in low prospecting activity.* But just what does "low activity" mean?

"Low" is an inherently unstable word. What's low for one individual or organization may not be problematic in another. From our perspective, low activity means *prospecting activity that is insufficient to sustain personal or organizational performance objectives.* In other words, you're not initiating contacts frequently enough to support a) your own career objectives, b) the potential of your market, or c) your organization's performance requirements. However you define "low," it always represents a pothole on your path to success.

The product definition of Call Reluctance is the one people most often intuitively rely on. But it's not enough to nail down a definitive diagnosis. Suppose you have a bad cough. You *might* have pneumonia. Or you could have just a cold. What difference does it make? Well, antibiotics can be prescribed to treat pneumonia, but they do nothing for the common cold. Same symptom, different treatment.

Similarly, low prospecting activity means you *could* have Call Reluctance. But it doesn't necessarily mean you do. There are other factors to consider. More than simply not hitting your prospecting targets, you should explore the *how* and the *why* of not making those calls. Without that information, you can't know if you're suffering from genuine Call Reluctance or something else entirely. Something that can't be treated like Call Reluctance, because it's not.

That's where the *process definition* of Call Reluctance comes in. It provides a systematic way to identify your specific prospecting problem. Authentic Call Reluctance requires the presence of three essential conditions: *motivation*, *goals*, and *goal-obstructive feelings.* We'll take a deep dive into those terms in a moment. If your prospecting activity is low and one of these conditions is missing or deficient, you're not call reluctant, you're dealing with a Call Reluctance *impostor.* Impostors mimic authentic Call Reluctance — that is, they can result in low prospecting activity. But they're not. Your course of action depends on your ability to tell one from the other.

Diagnosing authentic Call Reluctance involves taking measurements of these three critical components. These measurements reveal the current status of important emotional circuits that influence your prospecting. Let's examine these behavioral components and how they affect your ability to initiate contact on a consistent basis.

Motivation

Through years of use and exposure, "motivation" has become such a fluid term that no one can claim to own the exclusive description of what it is, what it does, and how it's expressed. Even academics who study it don't consistently define it. We don't claim to have cornered the market on the definition of motivation. The best we can do is offer a definition that serves our purpose. It's not necessarily the best or the most comprehensive, but in our case, it describes how motivation relates to Call Reluctance. Keep reading, and perhaps you'll agree with our reasoning for the definition we've evolved over time.

In the Call Reluctance process model, motivation is cognitive and physical energy available to support prospecting activity. From a mental and physical standpoint, it's the gas in your tank, the spark in your plug. Motivation isn't a metaphysical expression of your purpose on earth or your reason for getting up in the morning, not for our purposes. Some sources define it as exactly those things. And that may be appropriate in certain applications. But to explain the relationship between authentic Call Reluctance and impostors, we require the very narrow definition we present here.

Like any consistent, sustained activity, prospecting requires the mental and physical means to carry it out. Without that energy in reserve, contact initiation becomes an exercise in diminishing returns, like repeatedly cranking a car with a nearly dead battery and hearing the engine respond a little less enthusiastically each time.

We can break down your prospecting "battery" into three distinct components, any of which can become a drain on your motivation.

Amplitude

This is a measure of *how much* energy is available to the circuit that drives your prospecting activities. Some people naturally have more of it than others.

Others may have their energy impaired by physical factors — like illness, poor diet, or alcohol/drug dependency — or more insidious mental drains like lethargy or apathy. The outcome of trying to plug a low-powered salesperson into a high-powered sales career is the same as trying to charge a cellphone during a power brownout: The volts just aren't there.

Duration

Sustained prospecting activity requires uninterrupted access to a stable power supply. To continue the cellphone analogy, if you notice your battery is at 12 percent and you don't have access to a charger, you may try to "milk" the power by putting the phone in sleep mode and only peeking at it occasionally. But you may miss an important call or text because the phone wasn't up and running when it came in. Some salespeople take a similar approach to milking their energy. When it comes to prospecting, they perform only as long as necessary to "check in," or reach a certain level of productivity. Once that level is reached, they power down until the need to perform arises again. If you find yourself mimicking this peaks-and-valleys approach to prospecting, dedicating energy to it only for as long as minimally necessary, it's likely that your prospecting regularly drops below your potential.

Velocity

Some salespeople approach prospecting like the hare in the famous story, hitting the ground running and launching into contact initiation at breakneck speed. They may rack up great initial call numbers, but don't necessarily have a lot of stamina. Others are more like the tortoise: long-distance runners rather than sprinters. At any given point in time, their prospecting activity may appear less intense, even lethargic. Velocity is a stylistic difference that can help individuals and sales managers predict and account for patterns of performance.

Goals

Motivation is energy. Like electricity, which is also energy, it has to be connected to something in order to do its job. Electricity has the potential to transform your cellphone into a device that delivers entertaining podcasts and hilarious memes, but it needs to get there first.

Otherwise, you simply have a generic power supply and a dead phone. It needs to be plugged in.

Goals are the output device of your prospecting energy. They transform energy into action. The strength of your goals reflects the integrity of the connection. What's your motivation connected to? How reliable is the connection? Goal assessment is the process of finding out. Here's what to look for.

Target

This is what you want. It provides the meaning behind your prospecting efforts. Where do your motivational wires lead? What behaviors does your motivation support? Ideally, you should have clearly focused career goals that are supported by your prospecting activities. These goals should be accomplishable where you are now, not some other place, some other time. Motivation without clear goals becomes a mindless struggle without meaning; eventually, your drive overpowers your direction. Prospecting becomes mechanistic and tedious, boring you to sleep behind the wheel of your career. Contact initiation inevitably drops off.

Strategy

This is your plan of attack. Some salespeople take pride in being able to reel off their goals and ambitions at the drop of a hat to anyone who will listen. It impresses others and may even have helped them obtain their current sales position. But if you poke beneath the cover of their snappy patter, sometimes you don't find much else. No thought. No purpose. No planning. No meaning. Just easily remembered platitudes and empty ambitions recited for effect. Without a substantive plan for reaching your goals, you can easily get distracted, sidetracked, or just plain lost. One of the first performance areas to suffer the consequences is prospecting.

Pursuit

Just do it. Some salespeople define their targets and then spend endless hours constructing elaborate lists, plans, and strategies for reaching them. The trouble is, they rarely do anything else. They fail to devote sufficient motivational energy to actually completing the steps that would lead them to their goals. There's no target pursuit. Without pursuit, you'll never reach your goals.

Goal-Disruptive Feelings

The third dimension completes the Call Reluctance model. To be diagnosed as call reluctant, you must be motivated, goal-directed . . . and habitually disrupted by self-imposed mental obstacles when you attempt to prospect.

M   G
Motivation   Goal-Disruptive   Goal
                         Feeling

Back to our cellphone analogy. Goal-disruptive feelings are like data throttling. Your phone is fully charged. You have an "unlimited" data plan on a brand-new 5G network. But periodically your wireless carrier steps in and drops your connection speed to a level below what your device is capable of, for reasons that have nothing to do with you or the capabilities of the technology.

Call Reluctance does the same thing. It's an emotional throttle that disrupts the flow of motivational energy to clear goals. Energy designated for prospecting is diverted into fear-based prospecting *avoidance* behavior. Instead of supporting prospecting activity, it's redirected to recalling and reinforcing unproductive, possibly lifelong habits of escape and avoidance. Call Reluctance consists of all the thoughts, feelings, and actions that get in the way of initiating contact on a daily basis. Wishing, waiting, whining, and blaming are some indicators of call reluctant behavior.

The Great Impostors

When motivation and goals are derailed by fear, the result is sales Call Reluctance. When motivation or goals are missing or deficient, you also have a prospecting problem. But it's not due to Call Reluctance. It's an *impostor.*

Are you currently prospecting beneath your ability or potential? Are you call reluctant or are you dealing with an impostor? It's important to find out. Let's explore three of the most common impostors in more detail.

LOW MOTIVATION "ALL TALK, NO ACTION"

Some salespeople lack motivation. Some are motivated, but not enough to succeed in sales. What about you? If you're not prospecting because you don't have the energy to devote to consistent contact initiation, then you're not call reluctant; you simply lack the motivation. Your low activity might look like Call Reluctance, but the similarity ends there.

If you struggle with the Low Motivation Impostor, you probably don't really want to prospect, close, take responsibility for your personal growth, or tolerate the frustrations associated with it. You're not "reluctant" because you can't be afraid to do something you don't have the energy to do in the first place.

Note: Low motivation can't be "fixed" via goal-setting programs or sales incentives. Having clear goals is not the problem for these individuals. They could probably articulate exactly what they hope to achieve or attain in terms of their sales goals. The problem is, goals require a steady supply of focused energy to bring them to fruition, and they simply don't have it to give.

Why not? Low motivation can have one of two sources: physical or emotional. You may recognize one or both in yourself.

A person with physical Low Motivation may be a victim of poor health or poor health-management decisions. Illness, chronic conditions, detrimental lifestyle decisions, lack of exercise, and substance abuse can all deplete the amount of energy that could otherwise support contact initiation.

A Low Motivation individual of emotional persuasion, on the other hand, may have plenty of "gas in the tank," but it's continually diverted into unproductive emotions like apathy, disappointment, and indifference. This phenomenon is seen frequently in veteran salespeople who are tired of repeated letdowns from management or scattershot reorganizations that marginalize their years of service. Angry, demoralized, or both, they want to care, but their energy is disproportionately funneled into self-protection at the expense of self-promotion.

The thief of emotional energy can also come in the form of a major life event. Whether traumatic — the death of a loved one, an acrimonious divorce — or joyful — the birth of a child or an upcoming wedding — these times can be emotionally all-consuming. They command all the energy and attention that we have to give, and then some. And while the drain on our resources may be temporary, coping with these events in the moment often demands that we shift our motivation away from other concerns, including professional success.

If this applies to you right now, yet you're still striving to improve, kudos for attempting to keep things "normal"! Our only advice is: Don't try to be super-human. Being human is just fine, and natural. Keep reading if you find it helpful, or simply a useful distraction to help relieve emotional pressure. But we recommend that you delay actually applying any of the techniques in this book until you're less exhausted. They take energy, and you don't have any to spare right now. They'll be right here waiting for you when you're ready. Until then, we wish you all the best.

Outlook

The outlook for counteracting the Low Motivation Impostor depends upon whether the source is physical or emotional. If you suffer from low motivation due to apathetic indifference and can acknowledge your anger, then the outlook for corrective action can be very positive. This also depends on management acknowledging its own role in maintaining an angry, dispirited sales force, keeping its commitments, and being sensitive to the effects of corporate change on the sales force. Sometimes it takes the defection of top performers to less toxic competitors to make sales organizations see the harm caused by misguided policies.

If the cause of your low motivation is physical, then lifestyle changes are necessary to increase the energy supply available for career-related behaviors like prospecting. If you can't or won't make those changes, then you can't reasonably expect significant improvement.

Careerstyle

Here's what low motivation can look like. Do you see yourself in a number of these descriptions?

- You're satisfied with the way things are.
- You have little or no sense of urgency.
- You may enjoy rhetorical goal-setting, but make little behavioral investment in following through.

- You have a hard time understanding why managers take issues like marginal performance so seriously.
- You're satisfied with just getting by when it comes to reaching quotas.
- Your poor performance doesn't really bother you or spur you to make changes in your behavior.
- You often leave tasks or assignments unfinished, or finish them with erratic results.
- You're frequently late for meetings; when you show up, you frequently peek at your social media accounts on your phone.
- Your favorite part of attending conventions or professional gatherings is being entertained by humorous presenters, inspirational speakers, or anyone who doesn't make serious demands on your attention or intellect.
- You respond to external demands for increased productivity by ignoring the problem as long as possible, then changing companies.
- You can work hard, but typically only in short bursts.

Frequency of Occurrence

Low Motivation Impostors aren't uncommon. Some companies and industries have more than their fair share, such as financial services and construction sales. Overall, 23 percent of salespeople in the US lack enough energy to sustain their sales careers.

GOAL DIFFUSION "TOO MANY IRONS IN THE FIRE"

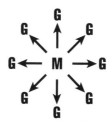

Do you make time for prospecting in your schedule? Do you balance daily professional and personal activities with a firm, written commitment to initiating contact with prospective clients? Or do you forge through your day, insanely busy, only to discover that it's too late to make prospecting calls?

Salespeople with Goal Diffusion are motivated. They have energy, but it's focused on too many other things besides prospecting. Online classes. Book club. Coaching soccer. Chaperoning the sixth-grade dance. Leg day (can't skip leg day). Goat yoga. Blogging about goat yoga.

Motivational energy is finite. To the degree that it's focused on other things (even if those things are worthwhile and rewarding in their own right), it's not available to support prospecting activity. Efforts to get in front of prospective buyers can't get off the ground because they can't compete with all the other interesting pursuits out there.

If this sounds like you, your prognosis is likely inertia: Starting much, completing little, interested in everything, mastering nothing. But you're not call reluctant. You can't be reluctant to do something *you're too busy to do.*

Goal Diffusion isn't a time-management issue. The

most successful salespeople on Earth have the same 24 hours per day as the least successful. The difference lies in how well successful people are able to prioritize what happens in those hours. For those living with the Goal Diffusion Impostor, it's not that they *can't* or *won't* prospect. Contact initiation simply doesn't land high enough on their to-do list to consistently be a priority.

Goal Diffusion has two common sources. The first is boredom, specifically the belief that boredom can't be tolerated and so it must always be avoided. Some people are sensation addicts, always looking for new experiences, fresh thrills, new sources of fulfillment. Their craving for engagement leads them to fill their lives with adventure of one kind or another. They may be compulsive volunteers or wannabe subject matter experts, TV binge-watchers or seminar stalwarts. Adrift in a sea of possibilities, they may find it difficult or impossible to firmly anchor themselves to a prospecting schedule when necessary.

The second source, for those in a corporate environment, is culture. Studies conducted with large, well-known organizations revealed massive Goal Diffusion scores within some companies' sales forces. Further inspection revealed that corporate policies, internal procedures, and endless recordkeeping protocols in these companies were cutting into the time, attention, and effort of their salespeople. These included the requirement to learn and utilize new software systems that were supposed to increase productivity but instead resulted in distracting and energy-sapping bouts of "technostress." With their attention fragmented, salespeople were unable to focus their energy on selling. When this was pointed out to senior management, no one accepted responsibility, and no one could remember exactly how it started. Like primordial ooze, it had simply evolved.

Slavish attention to I-dotting and T-crossing can result in frustration and rebellion where sales organizations want it least: among top sellers. Think about it. If you manage (or are) a rockstar producer, is a bit of sloppy recordkeeping a battle that really needs to be fought? Sure, procedures exist for a reason (usually), but at what cost? When Goal Diffusion is created and enforced through corporate policy, it needlessly stifles productivity, sometimes to the point that the rock stars start looking for a less restrictive environment to take their talents.

Outlook

When Goal Diffusion is a learned response to coping with boredom, and if you want to change, the outlook for refocusing your energy is extremely positive. When it's due to corporate culture, the ball is in management's court. Smart sales managers want to keep their salespeople, especially their top performers, happy and productive. If that means giving them more control over their priorities at the expense of perfect paperwork, savvy organizations, once made aware of the issue, are likely to do it.

Career Style

Here are some of the ways Goal Diffusion can appear. Do you relate to more than a few? If so, you may have the Goal Diffusion Impostor (and not Call Reluctance).

- You have energy, but not a lot of focus.
- You start a lot of projects, but fail to complete most of them.
- You tend to quickly lose interest in new pursuits and activities.
- You feel a restless, continuous need for novelty, stimulation, and change.
- You have a track record of frequently changing jobs.
- You're familiar with many subjects, but only on a superficial level.
- You have a good general overview of your product, service, and market, but you lack in-depth understanding.
- You tend to pursue many different interests, some of which conflict with your career goals.
- You may feel a loss of control because you're chronically over-committed.
- You consider yourself a self-starter, but if you're honest with yourself, your follow-through is poor.

Frequency of Occurrence

Goal Diffusion is common, but data analysis indicates an overall decrease in Goal Diffusion scores in recent years. This corresponds to an observed increase in Goal Level scores over the same period (see the Low Goal Impostor section next).

LOW GOALS

"All dressed up with nowhere to go"

Some salespeople have plenty of energy but don't know what to do with it. The connection between what they *do* and what they want to *accomplish* is corroded or incomplete.

Goals supply the focal point for your prospecting energy. When they're missing or murky, it's impossible to focus on (or even recognize) the things that are important. It becomes increasingly difficult to sustain initiative when you don't know or can't remember why you should be prospecting in the first place. When goals become blurred, self-promotion and self-advocacy become empty rituals, mechanical and soon discarded in favor of other things perceived as more rewarding.

It's important to recognize that quotas aren't goals. They're corporate objectives, targets you need to do reach keep your job. They're not what you should aspire to. Goals are a mission statement of *why* you do what you do. They should be personally meaningful and anchored to a desired outcome that transcends "hitting your numbers."

Low Goal Impostors have plenty of energy but nothing to plug it in to. If this describes you, you may find yourself struggling to find meaning in your career and a reason for working so hard. You may even borrow goals that seem to be working for other people and mindlessly channel your motivation toward them. Examples of borrowed goals include recognition, parental approval, status, and financial reward. These are all worthwhile goals, but if they're not *your* goals, the pressures of consistent prospecting in support of an outcome you don't believe in will eventually erode them away. When your goals no longer provide meaningful career direction, your prospecting activity will likely drop well below what it could or should be. That isn't Call Reluctance. You can't be reluctant to do something that you really don't want to do.

Origin

The Low Goal Impostor can originate from various sources. A small minority of those who struggle with it simply don't have goals, never have and never will. They're unable to direct their energy to anything that doesn't provide a short-term payback. These individuals lack fully functioning commitment faculties, a situation that ultimately may be traced back to brain structure or chemistry.

But the majority of folks who struggle with this issue never learned to define goals, select them and then strive toward them. This could be due to a lack of role models early in life: they didn't grow up around adults who had goals and purposefully worked toward them. It could also be because they weren't exposed to information or coursework focused on the life discipline of goal setting. This, however, appears to be a decreasingly common factor among younger generations of salespeople. In recent years, goal-setting has become an integral part of classroom studies in secondary schools and sometimes beginning informally as early as first grade.

Outlook

If low goals are due to lack of role models or exposure to goal-setting information, then the outlook is very positive, assuming you seek out the missing elements. It may also be useful to refine existing goals to make them more personally meaningful to you. For example, if one of your goals is "a six-figure income," but it doesn't seem to be spurring you on to positive action to reach it, consider redefining it in terms of *why* that income is important to you. What do you want to use it for? Early retirement? Longer vacations? Nicer things for your kids? This exercise may help you clarify goals you already have.

An international study of salespeople we conducted showed us some of the "whys" salespeople around the world embrace. In almost every country we surveyed, the chance to earn a high income was the #1 motivation for choosing a sales career, with the United States perhaps unsurprisingly leading the pack (55 percent of American salespeople named income as their primary reason for being in sales). But there were differences, as well. More than twice as many Australian sellers as Americans (25 percent vs. 11.5 percent) enjoyed the sense of accomplishment most of all. Among Canadians, the independence of a sales career was second only to income potential, the only group to list this factor among their top three motivating factors. Salespeople in Finland were the only ones to not choose income as their primary goal - they strongly preferred the lack of routine and sense of accomplishment they got from being in sales. As you define your goals, keep in mind that there really is no "wrong" target, and it definitely doesn't have to be monetary in nature.

Career Style

Let's take a look at what the Low Goal Impostor looks like. How many of the following describe you?

- Your prospecting activity typically gets off to a fast start, but soon settles down to a fixed plateau.
- You fail to prospect or self-promote consistently because you're consciously or subconsciously waiting for an opportunity to do something else (like changing careers or returning to school).
- You frequently monitor job postings, even if you're not actively engaged in a job search.
- You feel you're prone to job stress, burnout, or mid-life crisis.
- You find yourself exaggerating your loyalty to your job, your company, or your co-workers to disguise an ambivalent attitude toward them.
- You prefer workshops and books about positive attitude, motivation, and other topics that are ancillary to the topic of setting and striving toward focused goals.
- You get inspired by motivational presentations, but only briefly.
- You're easily distracted by relatively trivial issues

at work, like who has a nicer office, when the
next paid holiday is, or who is planning the next
company outing.

- You're unimpressed or unmotivated by
  incentives that seem to be reasonably effective in
  increasing other people's productivity.
- You get excited when new products or
  marketing materials become available, but your
  enthusiasm never seems to last long.
- You tend to talk long-term but act short-term.
- You need a lot of supervision and frequent
  reinforcement to stay focused on your
  objectives.
- You often act impulsively, without considering
  the long-term consequences of your actions.

Frequency of Occurrence

The result of the modern focus on goal-setting as a
skill to be taught alongside other academic subjects, is
an overall increase in Goal Level scores in assessments
of salespeople. This doesn't mean that the Low Goal
Impostor is likely to become extinct any time soon (some
people, for example, don't respond well to goal-setting
programs or aren't interested). Twenty-two percent of US
salespeople don't know why they want to prospect. But
it's encouraging evidence that exposure to the discipline
of goal-setting may have a positive impact on your ability
to define and pursue prospecting-related goals.

GOALS AND MOTIVATION:
HOW MUCH DO YOU REALLY NEED?

How important are clear goals and high motivation? What is the correlation between what we call "Big M" and "Big G" and your personal success? Our research suggests those relationships are important, but in a more complex manner than touted by some self-help books that insist upon crystal-clear goals and Olympic motivation levels.

Data gathered from several studies may help to clarify the issue. For example, Dudley and Goodson's 1988 study of the insurance industry's Million Dollar Round Table (MDRT) clearly showed that production was positively associated with goal levels, but within limits (see table). After a point, engaging in goal-clarifying activities actually interfered with production. Participants, who represented all MDRT production levels, completed the Call Reluctance Scale (SPQ*GOLD).

Top of the Table producers, the highest MDRT production category, averaged a Goal Clarity score of 64 percent on a 100 percent scale. The year these data were acquired, Top of the Table Membership required a minimum of $240,000 in commissions. Basic membership required only $40,000 and corresponded with an average Goal Clarity score of 46 percent. To express those numbers in modern dollars, 2018 Top of the Table membership requires $570,000 in commissions, and basic membership requires $95,000 in commissions. These are the creme de la creme of insurance sales professionals.

A non-MDRT comparison sample consisted of salespeople who represented the same companies and sold the same products at the same time and to the same markets as the MDRT sample. They also had approximately the same insurance sales experience. Their Goal Clarity scores averaged 39 percent.

MDRT GOAL LEVEL SCORES

Tier	Goal Level Score (%)	Production Requirement 1988	Production Requirement 2018
MDRT Top of the Table	64	$240,000	$570,000
MDRT (basic)	46	$40,000	$95,000
Non-MDRT	39	N/A	N/A

There is no question that for these samples, higher production is associated with clearer goals. The differences between these two groups are striking, but that's not the end of the story. The Top of the Table group, which included some of the highest-producing salespeople in the world, averaged only 64.11 percent. That certainly shows disciplined, daily management of goal-supporting energy, but it fails to support the fiction that high achievers are obsessive, "mission-driven," or have goals that are clearer than those of mortal men or women.

In subsequent interviews, we learned that many of the highest producers did not have three- or five-year plans. Many were uncertain even about what they wanted to accomplish in the next five weeks. And, in some cases, high producers were operating exclusively on a daily basis. A few knew what they were trying to accomplish, but had no discernable plan of attack.

Paradoxically, the producers who were most organized were the Over-Preparers (discussed on page 83) in the non-MDRT comparison group. They had everything organized and scheduled. These individuals kept neat lists, plans, charts, and schedules to project very lofty goals, but they had very little time to make calls and few results to justify the time they had invested in preparation.

Perhaps success in sales doesn't require heroic goals. The discipline to do the things that have to be done on a daily basis may be sufficient. If that's the case, then success becomes accessible to more of us, more often. That is truly unexpected and truly inspiring.

As part of the study, some of the Top of the Table producers brought up the role of religious faith in sales success. Religious faith was an important aspect of their career-management strategy, and they insisted that it be included in any explanation of their higher than average, but unspectacular, Goal Clarity scores. They reported that they conducted their daily affairs in the reasonable trust that their future is in better hands than their own.

"I just show up ready and trust the Lord to take care of the details," one said. To us, excessive planning and goal setting is a sign of Call Reluctance. To them, it shows a lack of faith.

Simplistic? They were some of the highest producers we've ever observed.

What about motivation? Motivation scores were also analyzed in the above study. Like Goal Clarity, High Motivation scores corresponded to high production and clearly distinguished the MDRT sample from the average producers in the comparison group. The Top of the Table producers averaged 74 percent on motivation, while the comparison group averaged only 42 percent. But like goal clarity, success in sales doesn't appear to require superhuman levels of motivation. The ability to consistently focus energy on daily goal-supporting behaviors like prospecting is more important than super-high motivation.

A FINAL WORD ON IMPOSTORS

This book is intended specifically to help identify and correct authentic Call Reluctance. It's for people who experience emotional short circuits that limit their ability to initiate contact on a consistent basis. There's simply not enough room in this volume to include corrective measures for impostors, or to present a comprehensive overview of the wealth of existing research into motivation and goals. We haven't even been able to list all the known impostors in these pages (like Call Reluctance, new types emerge as the research evolves).

A book dedicated to impostors is in the works, and we hope it will help the individuals who struggle with low motivation, low goals, and other issues. Until then, we urge you to seek out training, counseling, and advice from the many readily available resources as appropriate.

Finally, some salespeople who successfully address impostor issues discover Call Reluctance lurking beneath the surface. They bust through one set of barriers only to encounter another. Emotional roadblocks to prospecting that previously were obscured by low energy or unclear goals now come to light, keeping their prospecting levels suppressed even after other issues have been resolved. The good news is that these roadblocks can be overcome by applying Call Reluctance countermeasures. In chapter five we'll introduce you to these potentially career-changing procedures.

4

16 Faces of Call Reluctance

Some self-appointed sales "authorities" address Call Reluctance by downgrading it to simplistic clichés like "the fear of rejection" or "lack of confidence." A simple internet search shows this tendency to be long-standing and widespread among managers, trainers, and self-help gurus alike. The latter in particular often excel at ensuring their own job security by assuring salespeople that "no one escapes rejection" and that it "never goes away." And so the cliched diagnoses and bland "cures" persist, despite overwhelming objective evidence that the rocky mental landscape where Call Reluctance resides is more complex than previous generations of "experts" believed. Fortunately, serious modern practitioners of sales training have abandoned these discredited (but stubborn) labels in favor of more sophisticated methods of diagnosis and treatment.

When Dudley and Goodson initiated the first-ever serious Call Reluctance research in 1970, they too began under the misapprehension that it was a one-dimensional issue, like "shyness" or "timidity." But the idea that Call Reluctance could be reduced to such tidy labels soon collapsed under the weight of mounting scientific evidence. As we mentioned earlier, by 1986, when they published *The Psychology of Call Reluctance*, nine types of Call Reluctance had been identified. When the first edition of *Earning What You're Worth* was released in 1992, three more had come to light. Building upon the foundation of their discoveries, as of the publication of this book we know about 16 behaviorally distinct types. There may be more. Only time and additional analysis will tell.

Let's review what we've learned so far: To accomplish your career goals, you need to manage your visibility so that people who are in a position to recognize and reward your efforts know who you are. That means being an advocate for your success. *The fear of self-promotion* is the generic name given to an array of inhibitions associated with *initiating contact,* the critical first step in that process. When this collection of fear-based inhibitions specifically limits the ability of professional salespeople to prospect, it's known as *Call Reluctance.* Whether you're in traditional sales, consulting, politics, creative arts, or any other field that requires advocacy, the ability to comfortably, consistently initiate contact with new clients is necessary so that the other steps — *introducing* yourself, *informing* others (and being informed), and *influencing* a decision — can proceed to the outcome you desire (a closed sale, a promotion, etc.).

Decades of research have shown that there's no effective shortcut to assertive prospecting, no trendy sales gimmick that can take the place of consistent contact initiation. Regardless of your product, service, market, personal selling style, or economic conditions, the most reliable predictor of closed sales is the number of contacts you make with prospective clients. It's a powerful and empowering reality for those willing and able to embrace advocacy in their careers. Interestingly, in the course of questioning more than 200,000 salespeople about the factors they considered responsible for success or failure, two schools of thought emerged. A stunning 80 percent believed that success was the result of factors within their control, i.e., their prospecting activity and their personal attitude toward prospecting. The others attributed success (or lack thereof) to external forces like pricing, marketing support, and outside training — in other words, things they couldn't control (or weren't responsible for).

Not surprisingly, the second group, those who were more willing to make excuses and blame others, experienced higher levels of Call Reluctance. They habitually let their fears speak for them, and drown out their goals.

This chapter introduces the 16 faces of Call Reluctance in detail. For each type, we'll present a variety of descriptors, behavioral markers, and suggested countermeasures that can help you pinpoint your particular Call Reluctance issues and begin to overcome them (if that's what you decide you want to do).

We want to emphasize that the material in this chapter is not a substitute for professional assessment and specialized testing. Those tools are readily available from the publisher to those who want to take the next step. But they're not essential to begin your journey to proud, productive advocacy. Equipped with the information that follows, you'll be able to identify some of the attitudes and behaviors that could be interfering with your prospecting efforts. Recognizing the type(s) of Call Reluctance you're struggling with is the first and most important step you can take to correct it.

CHARACTERISTICS OF CALL RELUCTANCE

In earlier versions of Dudley and Goodson's work, the Call Reluctance types traditionally were presented more or less in the order they were discovered. It made sense to present them that way. First of all, it meant that the most established and extensively researched forms were spotlighted first, while newer types could be understood as building on earlier research. Secondly, it was just easier to add new types to the bottom of the list. Never underestimate the capacity of scientists to take the practical route whenever possible.

But in recent years we've evolved our approach. We recognize that not all fears are equal. Some are more generalized, tending to bleed into other areas of daily behavior besides prospecting, while others strike only under specific, limited circumstances. Still others affect parts of the sales process that occur *after* contact is initiated. These differences affect who is more prone to struggle with them, how they manifest themselves in various settings, and the best ways to counteract them.

As a result, we now place the 16 types of Call Reluctance into three "buckets": diffused types, targeted types, and secondary types. This arrangement doesn't reflect the importance or prevalence of each category. It simply allows us to talk about Call Reluctance less like a history lesson and more like the dynamic, cohesive discipline it is. Most call reluctant salespeople struggle with emotional short-circuits across more than one category. Fear is democratic that way.

Before we get into the types themselves, let's make an important distinction between productive and non-productive behaviors. Many forms of Call Reluctance start out as benign, even beneficial, behaviors. Over-Preparer Call Reluctance is a prime example. Obviously preparation and technical knowledge are useful, even necessary, when it comes to giving effective presentations. Being ready to answer client questions can give you a substantial edge over your competition. Those are all positive attributes. But if, over time or because of a negative past experience, you begin to believe that you *can't* or *won't* initiate a single contact unless you're completely prepared . . . that's when the positive desire stops being helpful and transforms into a stressful and expensive case of Over-Preparer Call Reluctance.

The same goes for other marker behaviors of Call Reluctance. Wanting to project a professional image, appear knowledgeable behind the podium, or avoid alienating friends and relatives doesn't make you call reluctant. It's only when these preferences harden into habits of escape and avoidance that they become a problem. They divert energy away from goal-supportive behaviors like contact initiation and into unproductive patterns of *coping* with prospecting. Waiting, whining, and blaming become costly alternatives to purposeful actions.

We will look at those patterns in more detail shorty. But first, here are capsule descriptions of the 16 faces of Call Reluctance discovered to date.

Diffused Types

Doomsayer

Your energy is frequently diverted away from initiating contact and toward over-vigilant anticipation of low-probability catastrophes. You habitually worry about the worst-case scenario and plan your prospecting activities around avoiding it.

Over-Preparer

Your energy tends to be over-invested in analyzing at the expense of prospecting. The time and effort you invest in preparation to make calls is excessive relative to the benefits you get by being *absolutely* prepared.

Hyper-Pro

Your energy is diverted to over-concern with projecting the *mannerisms* and *appearances* of success at the expense of goal-supporting behaviors like contact initiation. You may view "ordinary" prospecting as demeaning or unprofessional. You may tend to engage in the over-stylized use of professional jargon or name-dropping out of a reflexive need to appear better informed and more sophisticated than the "average" person.

Role Rejection

Your energy is squandered due to unexpressed and unresolved guilt and shame associated with being in sales (or being involved in selling or self-promotional activities). You may not be able to accept or affirm the worth of your career, which you may mask with a rigid insistence on appearing positive at all times.

Yielder

You habitually sacrifice opportunities due to a reflexive fear of being considered intrusive, pushy, or selfish by others. You often wait for "just the right time" to approach prospective buyers (which may not ever arrive). If you're in sales you may compensate for your emotional hesitation by rigidly adopting consultative, "soft" selling styles, which can elevate the importance of relationship-building at the expense of clientele-building.

Oppositional Reflex

You struggle with an ambivalent need for continuous feedback, which you then reflexively criticize and reject as invalid. You are emotionally unable to allow yourself to be coached, advised, managed, or trained. In the sales environment, instead of prospecting, you compulsively argue, make excuses, and blame others. Your knee-jerk reaction may be to disagree that any of this describes you due to the longstanding emotional barriers you've erected around yourself.

Targeted Types

Stage Fright
You habitually avoid or bypass opportunities to promote yourself through group presentations due to emotional discomfort with public speaking. Other forms of prospecting may be completely unaffected.

Social Self-Consciousness
Your energy is diverted to emotional hesitation to initiate contact with up-market prospective buyers. You tend to be intimidated by persons of wealth, prestige, or power. At times you may try to camouflage your discomfort by pretending outwardly that you don't care about any of those things while secretly struggling with feelings of inadequacy. Prospecting to other types of clients may remain unaffected.

Friendshield
You experience emotional resistance to mixing business interests with friendships. You find it difficult to prospect or self-promote among your personal friends or even to ask them for referrals. This can have adverse consequences even in sales settings where it's not necessary or appropriate to call on your friends.

Famshield
You experience emotional resistance to mixing business and family. You have difficulty prospecting for new business among accessible family members or asking them for referrals. This can have adverse consequences even in sales settings where it's not necessary or appropriate to call on your relatives.

Referral Aversion
Your energy is lost to emotional discomfort associated with asking existing clients for referrals. You may experience little or no distress when initiating new contacts, closing sales, or at other points in the sales cycle — but when it's time to ask for a referral, you hesitate, or don't ask at all.

Telephobia
You experience fear when trying to use the telephone for prospecting or self-promotional purposes. Face-to-face prospecting may be completely unimpaired.

Online Prospecting Discomfort
You struggle with discomfort using social media or web-based applications for prospecting or business development. You may over-rely on offline methods of communication even when you know they're less effective than technology-based solutions.

Complex Sales
Your energy is diverted to discomfort with prospecting and selling in environments that may require contacts

across geographical regions, multi-step approvals, or team selling. You may instead focus energies primarily or exclusively on simpler, one-on-one transactions.

Secondary Types

Sales Extensions

You're reluctant to approach existing customers about additional products and services you might be able to provide after the initial sale. Discomfort may focus on cross-selling, up-selling, on-selling, or a combination.

Close Reluctance

You experience emotional hesitation to engage in closing activities, such as naming price or asking for payment. You may over-emphasize customer rapport at the expense of assertively asking for an order or a decision.

A WORD ABOUT LABELS

Each of the Call Reluctance types is a basket of specific behaviors you may exhibit to cope with negative feelings about prospecting. A few of them are related to personality predispositions to some extent. But they're not personality types. Let's say that again: *They're not personality types.*

Call Reluctance doesn't define who you are, only what you do in specific situations. Some individuals, armed with the knowledge they gain from learning about the types, choose to label themselves or others: "Oh, I'm a Doomsayer!" "You're such a Hyper-Pro." "You just say that because you're Oppositional." We strongly recommend you resist easy verbal labels like these. They aren't useful for overcoming Call Reluctance and only reinforce the false idea that fear is somehow embedded in your DNA and can't be changed. Nothing could be further from the truth.

Here's why relying on labels is frustrating and counterproductive. Let's say you're at a friend's house, eating delicious burgers fresh off the grill. There's only one thing missing. You ask your friend for some ketchup. He goes to the pantry and takes out a squeeze bottle emblazoned with the familiar label of a popular ketchup brand. Without a second thought, you squirt the thick, red liquid onto your burger. But wait. As soon as you take the first bite, your mouth erupts like a volcano. Your tongue feels as if it's on fire. You immediately recognize the distinctive uber-spicy flavor of habanero peppers.

After drinking several glasses of water, eyes watering, you sputter, "What the heck? Dude, I asked for ketchup."

"That *is* ketchup," your friend says, unperturbed.

"No, it's not. It's habanero sauce."

"It's ketchup," he insists, picking up the bottle. "Look. What does the label say?"

You blink incredulously. "I don't care what the label says. At some point you poured habanero sauce in the bottle instead of ketchup. It's habanero sauce now."

He shrugs. "The label says ketchup, it must be ketchup. That's all I know. Deal with it."

The danger of labels is that they lead us to make assumptions about contents that may not be true. Identifying *anything* with a Heinz label as "ketchup" assumes that what's inside the bottle can't be changed. By the same token, branding yourself or others "a Yielder" presumes that attitudes and behaviors are fixed in an immutable pattern, defined by an arbitrary name. That's simply not true. You may cope with prospecting discomfort by habitually falling back on behaviors associated with Yielder Call Reluctance. But within that basket of Yielder-related habits, you have the ability to add, subtract, and alter them, now or in the future.

We occasionally slip into the convention of describing individuals this way ourselves, as a form of verbal shorthand. But we take care to never reduce a living, breathing, feeling person to a label that defines only one small part of who they are. When it comes to diagnosing and treating Call Reluctance, it's the contents we care about, not the labels.

DOOMSAYER

Even for a diffused type, Doomsayer Call Reluctance paints with a very broad brush. People who have it tend to be preoccupied with worst-case scenarios. They're not necessarily pessimists: It's not that they see the glass as half-empty, they're just worried that the glass will get knocked over and spill what's left.

Salespeople with Doomsayer Call Reluctance are always on guard against real or imagined (mostly imagined) dangers in their physical and emotional environment. For people in sales, that constant vigilance is a tremendous drain on emotional and physical energy that could be used to initiate contacts with prospective buyers. Instead of supporting prospecting, it circles the drain of low-probability catastrophes and is washed away.

The technical name for Doomsayer sums it up well: Threat sensitivity. People who are threat sensitive go through life in risk-assessment mode. If an outsider could see through their eyes, the view would likely resemble the screen in a first-person shooter video game: cluttered with gauges, statistics, and narration boxes that exist to help make moment-to-moment decisions about the safety of their surroundings.

If you suffer from Doomsayer Call Reluctance, you're probably familiar with the inner monologue of worry that characterizes this type: What if. . . , I'd better not. . . , Just in case. . . , Not worth it. You probably hear it every time you attempt to promote yourself or your interests. Do you let it guide you away from opportunities too often?

One study showed that Doomsayer Call Reluctance cost a whopping $27,600 annually in lost sales, the second highest financial impact of any of the 16 types in this case. Not surprisingly, however, it's uncommon among traditional salespeople. In a study of salespeople in 17 industries, Doomsayer wasn't among the most commonly observed type in any of them. In some (especially software/technology sales and hospitality), it's practically non-existent.

Why? The sales process, from prospecting to closing, inherently involves taking risks. People with Doomsayer tendencies don't gravitate naturally toward that role. Although they may be represented in any industry, they're probably most prevalent in careers that benefit from a native risk-averse orientation, like contingency planning or actuarial science. (Keep in mind that those positions still benefit from career-boosting advocacy, and Doomsayer can negatively affect the likelihood that such advocacy will occur.)

Here are some of the ways Doomsayer Call Reluctance can limit your ability to prospect and self-promote:

- Limited social involvement: You don't consistently put yourself where the clients/opportunities are.
- "Psychic Syndrome": You "just know" in advance who isn't going to be interested in your services and pre-emptively strike them from your contact list.
- Rigid behavior: You categorically reject engaging in certain activities, like cold-calling or networking events.

- Lowered expectations: You tend to define success as the absence of failure.

Where Does It Come From?

Doomsayer Call Reluctance can be learned from risk-averse managers and trainers. But studies are now beginning to confirm what some scholars and researchers have suspected for many years. Certain personality-based behaviors, like Doomsayer, also reflect a *hereditary* influence. Remember, while Call Reluctance isn't a personality type per se, your personality can predispose you to certain types. For many people with Doomsayer tendencies, their fear extends far beyond specifically initiating contact with prospective buyers. They tend to score highly on the personality trait "harm avoidance" on psychological tests, suggesting a predisposition to this type of Call Reluctance.

The Doomsayer Checklist ☑

If you agree with a number of these statements, you may suffer from Doomsayer Call Reluctance.

- ☐ I don't initiate contact with prospective clients as much as I know I should.
- ☐ Assertively promoting myself just doesn't seem worth the effort or risk of failure
- ☐ I avoid situations where I might be called upon to be spontaneous, witty, or "bubbly."
- ☐ When someone I'm talking to interrupts or

raises an objection, I have a hard time thinking on my feet in order to respond.

☐ I find it hard to praise myself or others. (True story: One of the authors, after giving her first-ever presentation on Call Reluctance, was asked how it went. Her response? "I wasn't as bad as the other guy!")

☐ Sometimes I find myself daydreaming about having daring adventures like "Indiana Jones" or jumping onstage at a comedy club on Open Mic night.

Can It Be Cured?

Because Doomsayer Call Reluctance can be influenced by unknown physical, chemical, and learning agents, it can only be contained. It's very difficult to "cure." The countermeasures in this book can help quiet the negative monologues and create more positive self-talk to support your goals.

THE FINAL WORD

"Avoiding danger is no safer in the long run
than outright exposure. The fearful
are caught as often as the bold."

— HELEN KELLER

OVER-PREPARER

Individuals with Over-Preparer Call Reluctance are easy to spot, in or out of the sales profession. They're the ones who lock themselves in their office before every meeting, feverishly Googling talking points and designing elaborate PowerPoint slides to back them up. They write multiple drafts of every email, even simple ones (few communications are "simple" in their mind). When completing written work, they cross every t and dot every i, no matter how long it takes. If someone cracks a joke or passionately defends an idea, they respond with restraint or skepticism.

Over-Preparer Call Reluctance occurs in people who cope with distress associated with prospecting by attempting to shut down those feelings entirely. Instead of allowing themselves to ever experience fear or anxiety, they channel it into meticulous preparation and technical precision. While there's nothing wrong with either preparation or precision, individuals with Over-Preparer tendencies take them to extremes, limiting their interactions with others to emotionally safe, information-bound channels. In sales, they tend to spend too much time preparing what to say and how to say it and too little time prospecting for people to present it to.

If you struggle with Over-Preparer Call Reluctance, you probably relate to feeling uncomfortable with initiating contact unless you have your presentation committed to memory, your supporting documentation meticulously organized and compiled, and the answers to all conceivable objections or questions at your fingertips. We were going to write "unless and *until*," but that implies a point in time when you feel completely ready. That point in time may not actually exist in your mind.

Over-Preparers tend to over-analyze and under-act. As a result, they have exhaustive knowledge of their product but no one to sell it to. Opportunities to initiate contact or advance the sales process may evaporate because they don't come at the time or in the form they had planned in advance. Being spontaneous or deviating from the script is too far out of their comfort zone to contemplate.

As a diffused type, Over-Preparer Call Reluctance tends to manifest itself in areas of life well outside the sales arena. Affected individuals typically are reserved, appear relatively unemotional, and respond with suspicion to "touchy-feely" people and philosophies. In general, they're not motivated by appeals to emotion or flashy displays of enthusiasm. They're far more comfortable in the realm of facts, procedures, logic and technology.

Despite outward appearances, however, salespeople with Over-Preparer Call Reluctance don't lack emotions or the ability to feel them. In fact, they may be easily overwhelmed by their emotions. Over-preparing is the behavioral response they've developed to cope with the intensity of their feelings. Facts and figures are the armor they don to do battle against a world that can seem too emotionally chaotic to handle.

If your prospecting activity is limited by your need to be absolutely prepared before you can comfortably initiate contact with prospective buyers, Over-Preparer Call Reluctance could be costing you money. How much? For one team of insurance salespeople, these tendencies cost them more than $1,900 per month, every month, in lost income.

But you're not alone. As the second most commonly reported type, it can be found in many industries, particularly those selling technical products and services, where its meticulous tendencies may seem to be a plus, but don't actually translate to positive sales numbers.

Here are some of the ways Over-Preparers can self-sabotage their efforts to prospect and self-promote:

- Failing to build rapport with clients
- Missing "buying signs" because they're too focused on giving their presentation exactly as written and in its entirety
- Burying prospective clients in supporting documentation and statistics while ignoring requests for an executive summary or 10,000-foot overview
- Not understanding the importance of creating excitement for their product or service
- Delaying or skipping appointments because of a minor typo or error in their presentation

Where Does It Come From?

Over-Preparer Call Reluctance is influenced by both heredity and early learning experiences. Some people with Over-Preparer tendencies may also have borderline obsessive-compulsive personalities, which are caused by a chemical imbalance in the brain. Still, we believe most Over-Preparer Call Reluctance is learned. It may be acquired from managers and trainers who have it themselves. It can also be the result of an early experience when lack of preparation caused negative consequences, resulting in an emotional over-reaction to the thought of ever repeating a similar experience.

The Over-Preparer Checklist ✔

If you agree with a number of these statements, you may suffer from Over-Preparer Call Reluctance.

☐ I don't prospect as much or as often as I should because it takes so long to get ready.

☐ I'm not good at off-the-cuff or spontaneous presentations.

☐ Pep talks and sales contests don't really motivate me to make more calls.

☐ If I notice that anything in my marketing materials is out of date, I'll wait until new ones are printed before I make another presentation. (This can also apply to resumes, portfolios, demos, etc.)

☐ I believe that if a prospective client has the maximum amount of information about my product or service, they'll make the logical decision and buy.

☐ I get frustrated when people want to make jokes and small talk when I'm trying to sell to them.

☐ If I make a mistake during a sales call, it takes me a while to get myself under control so I can continue.

Can It Be Cured?

Most cases of Over-Preparer Call Reluctance are preventable and correctable, given an accurate diagnosis, and proper training. But because of its invasive effect on the sales process, prevention is definitely the easier and more cost-effective route.

THE FINAL WORD

"In the workplace, we're taught to worry about what happens if we don't have full, complete knowledge of every detail. But if you create a culture and an environment that rewards people for taking risks, even if they don't succeed, you can start changing behavior."

— RESHMA SAUJANI, Founder of Girls Who Code

HYPER-PRO

Most reasonable people agree that active image management — "dress for the job you want," etc. — can contribute to success, especially in sales. But for individuals with Hyper-Pro Call Reluctance, projecting a professional image no longer furthers their goals. It becomes the goal. The quest for the perfect appearance ceases being instrumental and begins to interfere with what it was supposed to accomplish. It diverts energy earmarked for prospecting to a never-ending pursuit of the "right" image.

Hyper-Pro Call Reluctance occurs in salespeople who are trying to compensate for secret doubts they have about their worth and acceptability. To plead their case, that they are worth knowing and valuing, they affect the *appearances* and *mannerisms* of successful, accomplished people: Carefully curated wardrobes, status-symbol accessories (the latest phone, the most expensive handbag), expensively framed diplomas on every wall. Ostentatiously flashing the symbols of success, their motto is "If you can't love me, maybe you can love the Bugatti Chiron I drove here in." But the reality of their professional accomplishments seldom reflects the image they strive to project. Salespeople with Hyper-Pro tendencies are like paper dragons — flashy and impressive on the outside, but underneath just little kids running around in costume.

Like most types of Call Reluctance, Hyper-Pro behaviors typically start out as career-positive actions. Simply wanting to craft a successful image isn't a problem. It's the emotional investment in maintaining and protecting the image that does the real damage. If you struggle with Hyper-Pro Call Reluctance, you likely spend way too much time and energy defending yourself against real or imagined threats to your dignity. Like prospecting. To avoid being lumped together with shabby sales stereotypes, you may avoid "common" prospecting methods in favor of cultivating one or two high-value (but low-probability) clients — what we call "big case-itis." Or you rely on expensive, over-designed business cards to impress prospective clients. Or you name-drop obsessively, trying to create class by association. Anything to look like you've arrived, when actually you barely get up to speed.

In multiple studies we've found that the extra time and effort invested in image cultivation by salespeople with Hyper-Pro Call Reluctance doesn't pay off in increased sales. Many of them are average producers at best. What's more, preoccupation with the trappings of success may be less a ploy to dazzle clients than it is an attempt to convince themselves of their own credibility. We once had a client with an all-male sales team whose manager haughtily informed us (when we coyly suggested that they might favor Armani suits), "Oh, no, we only wear Brioni suits in our office!" (If you've never priced Brioni suits, prepare for sticker shock; they sell in the four- to five-figure range.) Impressive . . . except this team did 100 percent of their business on the telephone. Their clients and prospects never saw them in person, *ever*. So who were the expensive uniforms for?

Hyper-Pro Call Reluctance is vanity fighting against sanity. The placement and degree of vanities can vary among salespeople. Over the years, our studies showed us that Hyper-Pro Call Reluctance can take one of two slightly different forms, or the two can blend together. People with Hyper-Pro tendencies typically choose to spotlight either verbal or physical mannerisms to project their chosen image. We've christened those who primarily use verbal mechanisms as "Voice Proud." Those trying to project the image of success primarily through physical affectations are called "Appearance Proud."

Salespeople identified as Voice Proud focus on erudition and affectation. They like to hear themselves talk. People with elevated levels of Voice Proud Hyper-Pro enjoy using high-minded, multi-syllable words, some of which they may not fully understand. They may even deploy their ten-dollar words incorrectly; but whatever, it's the vibration of the air that counts. Their highfalutin vocabulary makes them sound intelligent (in their own minds). These folks also like to take up a lot of sonic space with words, drawing out syllables or developing quirky cadences to fill the atmosphere with their verbiage.

On the other hand, the Appearance Proud Hyper-Pro spends an exorbitant amount of time in front of mirrors, inspecting and honing their physical image. They comb, trim, preen, and tweak. To them, costume is more important than content; it's all about The Look. Flashy status symbols become extensions of the successful persona they need you to perceive in them. Cars, designer clothes, expensive wearable tech, cutting-edge business cards, and carefully curated accessories (they tend to "curate" items that most people simply "own") all combine to sell their image.

In either form, Hyper-Pro is the seventh most commonly observed type of Call Reluctance. In one insurance industry study, we found that salespeople with unmanaged Hyper-Pro tendencies averaged seven fewer prospecting calls per week than their less conflicted peers, the ones who allowed themselves to prospect no matter how they looked. That's well over 300 opportunities to make a sale defaulted every year to a preoccupation with appearances. In other words, all that extra effort into looking, sounding, and smelling like a success doesn't necessarily translate into more sales activity — or higher income.

Here are some of the ways Hyper Pro Call Reluctance can look (or sound) while it undermines your prospecting effectiveness:

- Obsessive interest in titles, degrees, and certifications (both what you have and what others don't)
- Needing to *always* be well-dressed and put together (no dropping the kids off at school in pajama pants, even if you don't get out of the car!)
- Tendency to pad conversations with factoids and minutiae about cars, wine, technology, art, and other "sophisticated" topics that have little to do with the objectives being discussed
- Habitual use of larger, more complex vocabulary than is necessary or appropriate for the audience
- Over-emphasis on making strong first impressions (and lack of follow-through after the first impression is made)
- Belief that style matters more than substance

Where Does It Come From?

Hyper-Pro Call Reluctance is largely learned. It tends to be prevalent among professionals who compete based on their "expertise," like financial advisers and, um, consulting psychologists (ahem). What about you? You may have had an early mentor who taught you that "image is everything." Maybe you once stumbled on a designer suit at an outlet mall and discovered that people seemed to treat you with more respect when you wore it (yes, that's taken directly from an episode of "The Simpsons," and yes, it happens in real life). Possibly there was a time when the approval of a loved one was dependent on whether you presented yourself in a certain manner. Someone taught you to cope with the opinions of other people in this particular way. Find them. Sue them.

The Hyper-Pro Checklist ☑

If you agree with a number of these statements, you may struggle with Hyper-Pro Call Reluctance:

- ☐ I don't take advantage of all the opportunities I have to prospect and self-promote.
- ☐ I can't do my job effectively when I think other people don't respect me.
- ☐ Over the years I've spent a lot of time and effort refining a certain image, and I expect it to be acknowledged.
- ☐ People usually decide to do business with me because they're impressed with the way I look and the things I know.

☐ It's important to me that people know the quality of person I am as soon as they meet me.

☐ I've been known to put off calling on someone because my outfit wasn't perfect.

☐ I often qualify my prospects by determining whether they're the kind of people I want to do business with.

☐ Prospecting and business development techniques used by most salespeople are inappropriate for me.

Can It Be Cured?

Is your image more important than your career? The outlook for Hyper-Pro Call Reluctance depends entirely upon self-responsibility. If you're willing to admit to yourself that you're letting affectations get in the way of real success, then the outlook is bright. The countermeasures in this book could be just what your career needs.

THE FINAL WORD

"But above all, in order to be, never try to seem."

— ALBERT CAMUS, *Notebooks, 1935-1951*

HYPER-PRO

Denial

We were working with a national company to help them determine whether or not they wanted to use our assessment for pre-hire testing of salespeople. Over several weeks, we went back and forth, providing information and what we hoped was persuasive evidence of its effectiveness. Finally, the head of Human Resources told us, "We need to work out whether prospecting is a priority for our salespeople."

Whether prospecting was a priority for salespeople.

Now, in our experience, HR professionals are typically prone to Hyper-Pro tendencies, with often a touch of Oppositional Reflex for good measure. That's certainly not always true, and we've worked with some great HR departments that had the smarts to truly partner with the people they serve and provide them with foundational tools for their success. Unfortunately, that wasn't the case here. We were dealing with an individual who had an emotional need to prioritize herself and her opinions over the productivity of the sales team.

There wasn't much we could do to overcome her attitude. So in the end, we waited. We waited for her to be fired, which didn't take very long. Afterward, the company sent two senior people to our management training workshop, and they subsequently began to use our assessment to find salespeople who would prospect.

ROLE REJECTION

Role Rejection Call Reluctance occurs in salespeople who are intellectually willing, but emotionally unable, to embrace a sales career. The weight of negative stereotypes about salespeople imposes a heavy burden on their daily activities. And fear of disapproval from loved ones, as well as their own unresolved feelings about accepting a sales role, exact an emotional and financial toll on their performance.

Even if they understand the opportunities available in sales and have the motivation and ability to succeed, salespeople with Role Rejection Call Reluctance *feel* like failures. They forbid themselves to integrate fully into their sales careers and ban real pride in their accomplishments from their emotional inventory. Instead, they pretend to be proud. To be positive. To be happy. All the while, negative feelings are sapping their energy and stifling their prospecting activity.

If you suffer from Role Rejection Call Reluctance, chances are you grapple with the feeling that you could be doing something better with your life, no matter how successful you are. Maybe you've been trying to come up with an alternative definition of what you do, one that doesn't include the word "sales." Have you thought about why you consider it necessary to do so?

Role Rejection is tricky to diagnose accurately because the afflicted salesperson may be unaware of the problem save for the nagging feeling that he or she should be considering a career change. Motivated and goal-directed, salespeople with Role Rejection Call Reluctance heroically strive to *appear* upbeat and optimistic, denying their doubts, making diagnosis more difficult. But their efforts to appear upbeat and happy when they feel doubtful and discouraged are usually foiled. Deeply entombed negative beliefs keep trying to scrabble to the surface: every salesperson is just a peddler; every sales career is inherently dishonorable; their sales career is a grim disappointment to their parents, friends and spouse.

The savage stereotype that has displaced their pride uncritically asserts that sales is an inherently dishonorable profession. Salespeople who succeed in a dishonorable profession are probably dishonorable too. How else could they succeed? They *should* fail, the stereotype insists. They *deserve* to fail.

Role Rejection can strike hard at non-salespeople, too, keeping a variety of contact-dependent careers from getting off the ground because of unsavory, unjustified connotations of "selling." Remember the list of advocates in chapter 1 — the job-seeker, the grant-chasing academic, the practice-expanding doctor, the entrepreneur? They all need, and deserve, to embrace the importance of *effective, ethical* prospecting to their jobs. Without shame or hesitation, they — like qualified salespeople everywhere — should feel pride in everything they do to succeed, including initiating contact with prospective buyers on a consistent daily basis.

No matter if you're new to sales or an accomplished veteran, Role Rejection can derail your career. It takes effort to deny and defend against persistent doubt about how you've chosen to make your living. Effort takes energy. Energy earmarked to smother unresolved guilt is no longer available for prospecting. With less and less energy available to fund prospecting, your clientele-building activities may well wink out of existence.

Role Rejection is the eighth most frequently occurring type of Call Reluctance overall. It tends to be most common in financial services — an environment in which salespeople are consistently encouraged to present themselves as educated, professional "advisers" rather than common salespeople. But it can be tremendously, unnecessarily damaging in any sales role. In fact, in a recent study we did with a residential real estate company, sales reps with high levels of Role Rejection earned about $36,000 per year less than their peers.

You may recognize some of the self-defeating behaviors that are the calling card of Role Rejection Call Reluctance, in yourself or others:

- Over-zealous use of self-help clichés and positive affirmations
- Use of deflected identities (like "relationship manager" or "consultant") to describe roles that are *primarily responsible for sales*
- Periodic episodes of career-related depression that aren't related to productivity
- Spoken or unspoken belief that most negative stereotypes about salespeople are true
- Hesitation to talk about what you do for a living at family or social gatherings

Where Does It Come From?

Role Rejection is 100 percent learned. Society has long supplied the exaggerated stereotypes that could predispose new salespeople to this form of Call Reluctance. All they need is a triggering device. That's supplied upon arrival. Unrealistic production quotas, unethical or shallow sales managers, negative stereotypes held by sales support personnel, and traumatic early sales training experiences can all summon Role Rejection Call Reluctance into being.

Most negative stereotypes about the sales career are communicated indirectly. The damage is inflicted subtly, but efficiently, by repetition.

One business writer explains the role of financial advisers this way:

> "When it comes to investments, retirements, and children's education, people want to work with a *professional adviser and not a sales person.* When an investment goes south, it is much easier for an adviser to calm the nerves of an investor than for a sales professional to accomplish the same task." (Emphasis added)

Meanwhile, a car dealership in Texas features this tagline prominently on its website: "No Sharks in Our Showroom!" It goes on to explain:

> " . . . [W]e do not have commissioned salesmen. In fact, we don't have salesmen at all! We call them Solution Specialists. Why do we do this? When we go shopping we want someone who will help us decide

what we want to buy, not *push or try to switch* us into purchasing something other than what we want to buy." (Emphasis added)

Finally, one of the more spectacular implosions in recent retail history occurred when former Apple executive Ron Johnson became the CEO of JC Penney in 2011. One of his first actions was to eliminate commissioned salespeople in all stores. A spokesperson explained, "Our new business model requires that we move away from a commission-based environment so that every team member is motivated by meeting the needs of our customers." (While this surely wasn't the only misstep that led to $4.3 billion in sales losses, it's notable that one of the first actions JCP took in the wake of Johnson's ouster was to reinstate commissioned salespeople.)

The spokesperson's statement, tellingly, reads like a Role Rejection Bingo card. Did you get "commission-based environment," "team member" and "meeting customers' needs"? If you did, put down your card and run. You don't want to win this jackpot.

Statements like these imply that earning commissions is somehow dishonest and automatically leads to unethical behavior. That's ridiculous. Commissions aren't self-centered. They don't lie, cheat, or steal. People do, if they choose to, and whether their livelihood is commission-based or not. If you believe — or allow yourself to be convinced — that people who work on commission are inherently selfish and dishonest, then you must believe that artists, Girl Scouts, and every successful self-employed person in the world is selfish and dishonest! There's no evidence that that's true. So why must it be true about commissioned sales?

These false but common beliefs all too often act as career poison. With every repetition and reinforcement of negative stereotypes, they etch deeper into the psyche of salespeople disposed to Role Rejection. Attitudes are slanted, biases are cast, productivity is diminished, career satisfaction is disallowed, and tenure is destroyed.

The Role Rejection Checklist ✔

If you agree with a number of these statements, you may suffer from Role Rejection Call Reluctance:

- ☐ I feel I've probably disappointed certain people by choosing a career in sales.
- ☐ At business and social events, I sometimes avoid telling other people what I do for a living.
- ☐ The negative images of salespeople in movies and TV shows prove that people think less of me for being in sales.
- ☐ I've been known to write upbeat blog posts or give uplifting speeches about sales, as much to boost my own attitude as anyone else's.
- ☐ The opportunity to make a lot of money got me into sales, but I'm not sure it's really worth it any more.
- ☐ Leaving the word "salesperson" off my business cards probably gives me an edge when I approach people.
- ☐ I spend more time reading books and articles

about emotional intelligence and having a positive attitude than those that cover sales techniques or technologies.

Can It Be Cured?

Role Rejection can be difficult to diagnose. (It's not diagnosed accurately — or at all — by most sales assessment techniques.) But once it has been accurately detected and measured, it's is among the easiest and fastest forms of Call Reluctance to correct.

THE FINAL WORD

"I've found that as long as you're fundamentally good — as long as you're not being bad to people — people give you a lot of room to be yourself, because being yourself is being honest. And that's what people want to see."

— ANDREW MASON,
Founder and Former CEO of Groupon

THE QWS SYNDROME

The QWS (Quit While Succeeding) syndrome is found in productive, veteran salespeople who unexpectedly abandon their sales careers. It happens when Role Rejection is ignored, neglected, and left unchallenged.

Call Reluctance is not just an affliction of inexperienced salespeople. It can strike at any point in a sales career. "Experts" who claim that conquering fear is simply a matter of getting a few successful calls under your belt are making a misinformed and damaging assumption. But they're not alone. Many sales managers (understandably) accept the outward appearance of success and career satisfaction at face value. After all, prior to dropping out, many QWS veterans enjoyed very high incomes. Some were the top producers in their companies. Some were the most productive salespeople in their industries. All were presumed by their managers and companies to be immune to annoying business development problems like Call Reluctance — until they abandoned their successful career, seemingly out of the blue.

In fact, QWS is the final, outward manifestation of an emotional conflict that built up over months and years. Call reluctant as neophytes, QWS salespeople were taught how to prospect but not how to do so comfortably. They learned the importance of projecting confidence without ever truly internalizing the worth and value of the sales career. Their abilities enabled them to be financially successful, but they never allowed themselves to take pride in their accomplishments.

Instead, these veteran producers learned to smother the problem by pretending to be positive, zealous and certain. Over time they took what they knew and amplified it.

Trying to reconcile their outward success with their inner emotional turmoil, many became desperate positivists, blogging about commitment, serving as speech-giving cheerleaders and challenging conventioneers to action. It was all theater. They allowed Role Rejection Call Reluctance to transform them into emotional frauds.

QWS salespeople share four common behavioral themes:

Denial: They drive their struggles underground, frantically coping with a problem they won't admit, even to themselves, is destroying their ability to go on. They never complain, or they complain about petty annoyances that don't seem to track with Call Reluctance issues. As a result, very few people — sales managers, close friends, colleagues or even family members — know Call Reluctance is a problem for QWS veteran producers, until they unexpectedly resign.

Compensatory prospecting: Their prospecting efforts shift away from emotional hot spots to paths of less resistance. QWS veterans may try to limit their internal turmoil by selling and reselling their existing clients. New accounts significantly decline.

Important market segments are bypassed. QWS salespeople may make unconvincing excuses for the shift in strategy to mask the purely emotional reasons behind it.

Career abandonment: Some veteran QWS producers leave the office on Friday afternoon with cheerful "have a great weekend" wishes for their colleagues, as they have so many times before, and simply never come back. After psychologically disassociating from the career, veteran QWS producers unexpectedly, and without warning, step completely out of character and resign. Leave. Walk away. To others, they seem to have impulsively quit the business many of them sincerely loved.

Post-mortem: The common explanation for their actions after the fact is eloquent in its simplicity, and one we've heard many times: "The financial return could no longer justify the emotional investment."

Among all the debris that Call Reluctance leaves in its wake, the QWS syndrome in veteran producers is the most damaging. It is also the most unnecessary. With a bit more sensitivity to the needs of experienced salespeople, this form of Call Reluctance could be eliminated.

YIELDER

Yielder Call Reluctance is easy to spot. It's the equivalent of the car that attempts to enter the freeway at 40 mph and then, nearing the end of the entry ramp, actually *slows down* as it tries to merge with much faster vehicles. It can't keep up, it won't speed up, and it practically crawls to a halt waiting for the moment when traffic will magically open up to let it in.

Like that slow, hesitant car, salespeople with Yielder Call Reluctance have difficulty asserting themselves, particularly when it comes to prospecting. They seek to avoid situations that require social risk-taking and actions that might bring about disapproval or conflict with others. Always tentative, rarely decisive, they tiptoe through their prospecting chores, waiting for an elusive magic moment to arrive.

If you have Yielder tendencies, you may possess an arsenal of behavioral techniques to avoid directly engaging with uncomfortable situations: procrastination, capitulation, busy work, small talk/jokes, hyper-agreeableness, retreat. While they may serve a short-term purpose of soothing your feelings of distress, they rarely move you closer to your goals.

Successful prospecting requires consistent contact initiation; it *is* an assertive act. For that very reason, it's troublesome for individuals with Yielder Call Reluctance. Afraid to bother the busy, disturb the indisposed, or interrupt the otherwise engaged, they become obstinately inactive, waiting for just the right time and circumstances to make the call or visit the prospect. Not surprisingly, opportunities fly by while they remain rooted in place.

If your career depends upon advocacy — your willingness to prospect, self-promote, network, lobby, or otherwise assert yourself to others — Yielder Call Reluctance can make you an also-ran in the race to success. To the degree that you're preoccupied with the *perceived* consequences of offending or intruding on people, you're likely sacrificing your career interests to the interests of others on a daily basis.

Yielder is the most commonly observed form of Call Reluctance, regardless of industry, sales setting, or location. It's especially common in sales organizations that have adopted a "consultative" or "relationship-based" model, which is attractive to salespeople with Yielder Call Reluctance and can actually teach conflict-avoidant attitudes to salespeople who didn't previously exhibit them. Yielder Call Reluctance is also among the most costly types: a study of insurance salespeople found that those with Yielder tendencies lost almost $33,000 in potential income per year to their fear of assertive prospecting.

Here are some of the behavioral calling cards of those who struggle with Yielder Call Reluctance:

- Overemphasizes rapport-building elements of the sales/advocacy process at the expense of assertive prospecting and closing
- Relies on non-threatening, indirect forms of contact initiation (email, collecting business cards, etc.), but fails to follow up on leads
- Is easily deterred by failure or rejection and

takes a lot of time to recover emotionally —
time that could be used to initiate more contacts

- Considers assertive people to be aggressive and
  unprofessional
- Doesn't simply hesitate, but rigidly *refuses* to be
  assertive; becomes indignant at the suggestion
- Lets anger build up inside because expressing it
  openly is "inappropriate"

People with Yielder Call Reluctance cope with emotional discomfort by avoiding interpersonal conflict and
behavior that might be seen as "aggressive." As a result,
they may appear on the surface to be mild, easygoing,
even timid. But make no mistake: Salespeople with
Yielder Call Reluctance are not the opposite of the stereotypical swaggering, high-pressure salesperson. Many
are in fact rigid in their insistence on being seen as the
nice guy. They can be as ruthlessly committed to their
meek persona as any pushy sales stereotype.

Individuals with Yielder Call Reluctance, frustrated
with their inability to assert themselves over others, may
simply drive their thwarted ambitions underground. For
some, energy-sapping discomfort undergoes a fermen-
tation process and distills into anger, which is equally
or more destructive to a productive career. Smiling
and solicitous on the surface, they engage in gossip and
behind-the-scenes power plays to attempt to control their
surroundings. In performance reviews, they may eagerly
agree with everything their manager says, including that
they need to make more calls, then proceed to make
no changes to their behavior whatsoever until the next

review, when they once again eagerly agree they need to make more calls. Their sincerity during the meetings is so convincing that this process may be repeated over a long period of time, until management finally tires of funding a pleasant non-producer.

Where Does It Come From?

Yielder Call Reluctance can result from several influences:

1. **Exposure to Yielder beliefs:** Sales trainers, training materials, and entire organizations can be contaminated with Yielder Call Reluctance. This is often evidenced by a reliance on "soft-sell" or "relationship-based" techniques that characterize "traditional" selling as unprofessional and ineffective. These beliefs do more to spread Yielder Call Reluctance than all other influences combined.

2. **Heredity**: This type is related to the general personality trait of low dominance. When a person with low dominance enters the sales profession (or any professional situation that requires consistent assertiveness), Yielder Call Reluctance can bubble up to the surface.

3. **Past experience**: Some families and some cultures actively encourage a negative attitude toward intrepid self-interest. Traits like modesty and humility are promoted over assertiveness and self-confidence, which may be disparaged as seeming

pushy and boastful. Those deeply ingrained messages can be difficult to shake, even when common sense disputes them and success depends on doing so. (You *can* be humble, assertive, modest, and confident all at the same time.)

4. **Societal expectations**: We've found that women tend to struggle with Yielder Call Reluctance more than men. This is likely due to generations of women being discouraged from exhibiting "masculine" traits like assertiveness and encouraged to be more "warm" and "nurturing" instead. Formal and informal research studies suggest, for example, that women are less likely to ask for raises than men and to negotiate salaries and perks during the hiring process. (See Appendix A for more information about gender differences.)

The Yielder Checklist ☑

If you agree with a number of these statements, you may suffer from Yielder Call Reluctance:

- ☐ I don't initiate contacts with prospective buyers as much as I could or should relative to my goals.
- ☐ I frequently put off making calls by convincing myself it's a bad time for the client.
- ☐ I tend to give up too quickly when someone says they're not interested in my product or service.
- ☐ If I do a good job of connecting emotionally with a prospective client, they'll want to do

business with me instead of someone who only talks about features and price.

☐ Sometimes I feel as if other people are taking advantage of me, but I rarely push back or defend my own interests.

☐ I tend to offer to drop the price before my prospect expresses any concern about it.

☐ When I receive a rejection or a harsh critique, I find myself composing forceful, eloquent comebacks in my head, hours, or days after the fact.

Can It Be Cured?

The outlook for correcting Yielder Call Reluctance can be very positive. When it's properly assessed and the appropriate training procedures are used, it can be quickly contained and prospecting performance can be markedly improved. NOTE: Very high levels of Yielder are more difficult to correct because deeply entrenched fears will fight to survive, no matter what it takes. If you struggle with moderate-to-high levels of Yielder Call Reluctance, you may reflexively, enthusiastically agree with critiques or helpful advice (like this!) without any follow-through. Rhetorical agreement acts as a shield to protect yourself from the emotionally challenging process of actually changing your behavior. These tendencies can be reined in *IF* you can allow yourself to admit there's a problem — and do something about it.

Although the countermeasures described later in this book are helpful for Yielder Call Reluctance, basic assertion training can be helpful, too. Assertion Training isn't included as a countermeasure in this book because it's readily available elsewhere. One of the best books on the topic is *Your Perfect Right* by Robert Alberti, PhD and Michael Emmons, PhD. Although it doesn't deal directly with Call Reluctance, it's an excellent introduction to the problems associated with low assertiveness. Women may want to check out *Just Ask for It* by Linda Babcock and Sara Laschever to improve their confidence and negotiating skills.

THE FINAL WORD

"The best gifts are never given, but claimed."

— WARREN ELLIS, Author

OPPOSITIONAL REFLEX

Some forms of Call Reluctance are quiet. They whisper in your ear and nibble at your confidence. For the most part, they're private, unspoken fears that do their damaging work in the hidden recesses of your mind.

Not Oppositional Reflex Call Reluctance. It's big, and it's noisy, and it wants everyone to know it's around. At that task it generally succeeds. Even if you don't know it by its name, you probably recognize the behaviors of Oppositional Reflex when you see them in other people.

And that's the crux of the problem. If you have Oppositional Reflex Call Reluctance, there's little chance that you'll see *yourself* in the following description. But keep reading anyway.

In meetings, these individuals present themselves as the subject matter expert, no matter what the topic is. In training, they make sure everyone knows if they're bored or they disagree with the instructor. During performance reviews, they blame less-than-stellar sales numbers on the product, the customers, management, the company website — anything but their own lack of productivity.

Salespeople with Oppositional Reflex Call Reluctance habitually speak when they should be listening, instruct when they should be learning, criticize when they should be commending, reject when they should be accepting. They boast that they're the smartest, the strongest, and the best (at everything!) while discrediting the methods, contributions, and achievements of everybody else.

Like all Call Reluctance, Oppositional Reflex is a behavioral response developed to cope with fear. Despite strutting about with bombastic self-certainty, Oppositional Reflex actually guards a bruised, embattled psyche that probably decided — perhaps years ago — that no one can be trusted and the only option left is to fight. Dedicated to appearing independent, self-reliant, and complete, these individuals usually do the *exact opposite* of what they are asked to do. They simply can't allow themselves to be coached, advised, instructed, managed, or trained.

Ignoring their talents and discarding their dreams, they swell the ranks of malcontented, underachieving salespeople. Unable to be taught, they never learn how to prospect successfully, manage their sales career, or control their frustrations. Bursting with promise, but bound to righteous indignation, salespeople with Oppositional Reflex Call Reluctance may rarely reach their goals or realize their potential.

Oppositional Reflex doesn't necessarily make it impossible to have a successful sales career. After all, there will always be some customers who essentially allow themselves to be bullied into making a purchase. But they're unlikely to remain customers for long. Eventually, many salespeople with Oppositional Reflex find themselves unwelcome in their clients' offices — and, with their customer base shrinking, in their own.

If you're a salesperson with Oppositional Reflex, at this point you're mentally finding fault, denying you have Call Reluctance, making excuses, and rebuffing our efforts to help you, just like every other time someone tried to help you. But take heart. This time could be different. Look, you're still reading. Is a small part of you ready to consider making some big, positive changes? Pause for a moment. Listen to yourself — carefully. Then, for once, lay down your weapons.

Oppositional Reflex is the fourteenth most frequently observed type of Call Reluctance. It's most prevalent in psychologists, psychiatrists, and academics. Consultants and inspirational speakers often have it in massive doses, which is why they tend to drift into careers that allow them to be self-employed "experts."

Here are some of the energy-draining behaviors common to Oppositional Reflex Call Reluctance:

- Saying "no" far more often than "yes"
- Picking fights over minor issues simply to be proven right
- Finding fault with everything except themselves (price point, sales supports, market conditions, management's "incompetence")
- Experiencing emotional blowups, often followed by half-hearted apologies and temporary remorse (until the next blowup)

Where Does It Come From?

The capacity of Oppositional people to agitate quickly, intensely, and frequently is probably due to hereditary factors. But hereditary tendencies don't necessarily translate into full-blown Oppositional Reflex Call Reluctance. That has to be learned, practiced, and refined.

Salespeople with Oppositional Reflex typically have personal histories of traumatic disappointment, misplaced trust, or unrequited affection. Striking back and resisting was how they chose to save face and cope. Repeated countless times since then, in countless circumstances, resistance has been honed and polished into an overpowering behavioral weapon. Sovereign and autonomous, it now controls them.

The Oppositional Reflex Checklist ☑

If you agree with a number of these statements, you may struggle with Oppositional Reflex Call Reluctance. Note: If you reject every statement out of hand, and get annoyed doing it, consider reading through the list one more time and *honestly* deciding whether the items might pertain to you.

- ☐ I don't feel as if I'm as productive or as successful as I could be.
- ☐ When I'm in a group of people, I instinctively say and do things that make me the center of attention.
- ☐ I don't listen closely to others because I usually start forming a rebuttal or comeback in my head as soon as they begin speaking.
- ☐ It's important to me to always have the last word in a debate, argument, or even just in casual conversation.
- ☐ It's hard to get anything done in my job because no one except me knows what they're doing.
- ☐ People say I don't follow instructions, but the truth is my way of doing things is almost always better than anybody else's.

☐ Many of the choices I make in my career are motivated by the desire to get back at people who have wronged me.

☐ I don't feel the need to be polite to people who are wasting my time. I'll interrupt a speaker or walk out of a class if I have to.

Can It Be Cured?

Is winning senseless arguments more important to you than accomplishing your goals? Is it more important than earning what you're worth?

The outlook for this type of Call Reluctance depends upon your answers. If you can admit to yourself (and others) that you probably have Oppositional Reflex, then you've already taken the first, and most difficult, step. For you, the outlook is promising and bright. Change should come quickly. The outlook is murky if you can't — or won't. Even so, if you're growing restless with meaningless arguments, transparent excuses, casting blame, and denying responsibility, the countermeasures in this book could be just what your career needs. Why not give them a chance?

THE FINAL WORD

"Anger is fear's bodyguard."

— CELESTE NG, *Little Fires Everywhere*

AN OPPOSITIONAL STORY

At a recent industry convention, a gentleman approached our booth and demanded, "Who's the most senior person here?!" He clearly wanted to talk to the person in charge, but he was also putting off a real "YOU BETTER TAKE ME SERIOUSLY" vibe, so we asked, "You mean by age?" and pointed to the gray-haired guy in the booth with us (one of our longtime distributors). We were trying to lighten him up a little. Didn't work.

Again, he demanded the most senior person. Co-author and company CEO Suzanne Dudley introduced herself and asked what she could do for him. He stated that *his* recruitment process knocked out 80 percent of the people who applied for a position with his company. Of the rest, "If they don't call, they don't stay. Period." He triumphantly added, "So tell me why I should use your test."

Dudley inquired, "Well, how much does it cost you to make a bad hire?"

"Nothing," he sneered. "If they don't call, they're gone immediately. So WHY SHOULD I USE YOUR TEST?"

By this time, it was very clear to Dudley what she was dealing with. His puffed-up self-certainty, demands for attention, and sneering dismissal of ideas other than his own were all classic marker behaviors of Oppositional Reflex. So, Dudley stopped pretending she was dealing with a rational person inquiring to see if our offerings could help his business. She switched into dealing-with-Oppositionality mode, what we call "unplugging."

"It sounds like your process is pretty good just the way you have it. If you do make a hiring mistake, it's not costing you anything, so you probably DON'T need our assessment," she said.

His body language changed instantly, although clearly he was slightly befuddled by our cheerful capitulation to his bluster. Now calmer and more relaxed, he replied, "Well, explain to me what your assessment does." Dudley went through the standard pitch, explaining how our assessment is different from personality tests, how "prospecting" is more than just cold calling or using the phone, etc.

After she finished, he went back to his former dominant, commanding posture. And he demanded, "Who here is going to follow up with me? WHO IS GOING TO CALL ME NEXT WEEK?" And Dudley pointed at the gray-haired guy next to her.

In our experience, beneath their belligerent swagger, many folks with Oppositional Reflex just want to be heard, but their only interpersonal tools are blunt-force instruments. The ones who can allow themselves to stop swinging long enough to listen can often experience remarkable transformations, in themselves and the teams they hire and manage.

STAGE FRIGHT

Of all the Call Reluctance types, Stage Fright may be the most familiar to those who don't consider themselves to be "in sales." Discomfort with public speaking is the most commonly reported fear among the general population, beating out flying, heights, and spiders. (Yes, even spiders.)

Among salespeople, Stage Fright is a targeted fear that affects their ability to comfortably prospect to groups of people. This may include making "seminar selling" presentations, leading "lunch and learn" sessions, or attempting to close a sale before multiple decision-makers. We've even gathered anecdotal evidence that Stage Fright can affect individuals working in call centers or "bullpens," who may become anxious at the thought that those around them can overhear (and judge) their calls.

If you suffer from Stage Fright Call Reluctance, it may affect only your ability to speak before large groups. Or only small groups. You may not feel comfortable presenting to groups of any size. And your willingness to prospect one-on-one may be completely unaffected.

We used to think that the discomfort experienced by salespeople with Stage Fright had a singular cause: They felt over-anxious about their physical appearance and how it was perceived by others. We've since learned that isn't necessarily the case. Like Hyper-Pro Call Reluctance, Stage Fright isn't one-dimensional. There are two discernible types.

The first, Image Concern, centers on the body. It's identifiable by intense focus on physical appearance. A salesperson with this strain of Stage Fright feels uncomfortable knowing that everyone will be *looking* at them. Their self-talk relentlessly harps on real or imagined dangers associated with this physical scrutiny: Did I remember to zip my fly? Am I dressed appropriately? How's my hair? Please don't let me trip on my way to the podium!

On the other hand, some people with Stage Fright aren't concerned about their appearance at all. Instead they have Content Concern. They're preoccupied with the possibility of saying something that would sound ignorant, superficial, or foolish. They emotionally unravel at the thought that everyone will be *listening* to them: What if my mind goes blank? Will they think I don't know what I'm talking about? Whatever you do, don't stammer. This concern isn't necessarily related to actual expertise. Legendary singer/actor Barbra Streisand famously avoided public performances for *30 years* after forgetting the lyrics to a song during a concert in 1967.

If you have opportunities to reach prospective customers via group presentations, Stage Fright Call Reluctance can shut them down. If you work in an industry where "seminar selling" is expected or required, it can be catastrophic.

We found the highest level of Stage Fright Call Reluctance in the financial services industry. About 42 percent of the hundreds of thousands of financial services salespeople that we've assessed are uncomfortable speaking in front of groups. When we crunch the numbers, that translates to an estimated $10,000 of lost revenue per year per salesperson with Stage Fright!

Here are just a few of the advocacy scenarios that may be threatened or shut down by Stage Fright:

- Authors promoting a new book via radio or TV interviews
- Consultants speaking to industry groups or conventions
- Entrepreneurs giving sales parties to sell housewares, makeup, clothing, etc.
- Financial advisors hosting seminars to introduce retirement plan options
- Community activists appearing before the city council to support or oppose a ballot issue

Where Does It Come From?

Stage Fright Call Reluctance appears to be entirely learned. It may result from inexperience as a group speaker or from an early traumatic experience associated with public speaking. Comedian and actor Jim Carrey was viciously heckled during his first on-stage experience as a teenager; it was two years before he could make a second attempt. Obviously, he eventually overcame that negative experience. Can you afford to take two years to recover between group presentations in *your* career?

Negative attitudes about public speaking can also be absorbed from people who themselves suffer from Stage Fright and assume everyone else does, too — for example, a mother who says, "Pretend the audience is in their underwear and you won't be so scared!" before little Johnny performs his starring role in the kindergarten musical. Little Johnny probably wasn't afraid until his mother intimated that there was something to be afraid of! (Quite possibly an audience full of people in their underwear?!)

The Stage Fright Checklist ☑

If you agree with a number of these statements, you may suffer from Stage Fright Call Reluctance.

- ☐ My product or service lends itself to group presentations or "party sales."
- ☐ I don't make as many group presentations as other, more successful people in my line of work.
- ☐ I begin to get nervous and stressed out just thinking about public speaking.
- ☐ When I have a group presentation coming up, I obsess over the details days or weeks in advance.
- ☐ I don't like the way my voice sounds, even to myself.
- ☐ Ice-breaking and role-playing exercises are among my least favorite things.
- ☐ When I do speak to a group, I probably come off as stiff and over-rehearsed, because that's how I feel
- ☐ There are so many gifted public speakers that even if I were comfortable making more group presentations, I'm sure I wouldn't be nearly as effective as they are.

Can It Be Cured?

Stage Fright can be among the easiest forms of Call Reluctance to correct, assuming it's been properly assessed. Cognitive approaches, which gradually decrease distress, have proven successful. Many researchers are also looking into 21st-century adaptations of these techniques employing virtual reality. The countermeasures you'll find later in this book, especially Sensory Injection, can be extremely helpful.

THE FINAL WORD

"It's interesting — years ago, I had such bad stage fright during musical theater auditions that I just gave up. And now I'm on Broadway."

— TOM LENK, Actor

SOCIAL SELF-CONSCIOUSNESS

Social Self-Consciousness Call Reluctance manifests itself in a very specific set of behaviors. In reaction to emotional discomfort inspired by a certain type of prospect, sufferers employ the opposite of target marketing: target *avoidance.*

Some salespeople with Social Self-Consciousness Call Reluctance complicate matters by insisting they're not call reluctant at all. According to them, they can initiate contact with *anyone* — unless, of course, their prospect fits into a group they have emotionally targeted to exclude from their market. Typically, salespeople with Social Self-Consciousness Call Reluctance shun prospects who have wealth, prestige, power, education or social standing. They find these groups intimidating, even threatening, and so they summarily dismiss up-market clients from their prospecting radar.

If you suffer from Social Self-Consciousness Call Reluctance, you may not experience discomfort with any particular method of prospecting or selling style. Your hesitation to initiate contact is primarily centered not on *how,* but on *who* — in this case, wealthy, powerful, or prestigious buyers.

Social Self-Consciousness can be extremely limiting. When a company shifts its marketing emphasis to up-market clients; or when purchasing decisions for a product or service are made at high organizational levels; or when educated, professional people constitute the prime market for a product or service, it can be lethal to a sales career.

Salespeople with Social Self-Consciousness Call Reluctance cope in a variety of ways. They may become defensive when asked why they won't target up-market prospects. Some pretend to be dismissive of wealthy, powerful people in general to disguise a belief that they don't measure up. Others over-invest in motivational and esteem-building programs to try to combat feelings of intimidation.

An unfortunate behavior displayed by some Socially Self-Conscious salespeople is to be rude and verbally abusive to people they perceive to be lower on the social totem pole than they are. They look down on service people, blue-collar workers, wait staff and the like, just as they believe they're looked down upon by CEOs, doctors, business leaders, etc.

There's a famous, oft-repeated quote by humorist Dave Barry: "A person who is nice to you but rude to the waiter is not a nice person." Maybe. Or maybe they're displaying a classic marker behavior of Social Self-Consciousness. Whether or not they're a nice person is probably better left to discussions on Reddit.

If you're shackled by self-inflicted emotional boundaries caused by Social Self-Consciousness Call Reluctance, you may (consciously or unconsciously) be prohibiting yourself from prospecting across the entire social spectrum. This may not be a problem if you're selling, say, office supplies or Girl Scout Cookies. But if your success depends on initiating contact with CEOs, civic leaders or up-market buyers, it can impose a significant limit on contact initiation and throttle the sales process from the outset.

Self-Consciousness Call Reluctance limits sales performance only in industries where calling on up-market contacts is required, and it's among the least frequently observed types. However, in a recent study using our latest Call Reluctance assessment (the SPQ*GOLD/ Full Spectrum Advocacy) we found that over 40 percent of people in the financial services industry struggle with it. Presumably these individuals are content prospecting among the low-hanging fruit, defaulting the higher commissions that come from selling to the people with the greatest wherewithal to invest to less conflicted competitors.

Here are some of the ways your career can be affected by Social Self-Consciousness:

- You continually need to book more, lower-margin sales because you avoid prospects who could award larger contracts.
- You waste time giving sales presentations to individuals who aren't empowered to say yes or authorize payment.
- You include wealthy and powerful people in your prospecting strategy, but find ways to avoid actually contacting them.
- You spend time and money acquiring multiple certifications, titles, etc. in an attempt to feel "worthy" to initiate contact with up-market buyers.
- You squander energy feeling angry at wealthy prospects for intimidating you (and at yourself for feeling intimidated), leaving you without the "juice" to pursue more business.

Where Does It Come From?

No one is born with Social Self-Consciousness Call Reluctance. It's learned, highly contagious and easily acquired, usually through passive learning. For some, it can be the result of growing up in a blue-collar environment, hearing attitude-shaping opinions about "us" and "them" that carry over into adulthood. In the corporate environment, it can be carried by sales managers, consultants or training materials whose authors project their own emotional hesitation onto unsuspecting trainees. Often, because of the particular coping behaviors associated with it, it is confused with low self-esteem and low assertiveness, which are more related to other forms of Call Reluctance.

The Social Self-Consciousness Checklist ☑

If you agree with a number of these statements, you may suffer from Social Self-Consciousness Call Reluctance.

- ☐ Upscale buyers, business and civic leaders, and high-level professionals are a good market for my product or service.
- ☐ My career would really benefit from doing more business with up-market clientele.
- ☐ I don't initiate contact with those kinds of buyers/decision-makers as often as I could or should.
- ☐ There are people in my professional/social circle I could probably sell to, but I'm too intimidated by them to attempt it.

- [ ] Sometimes I feel that I'm not good enough to approach some kinds of prospects.
- [ ] I'm good at making excuses for avoiding or procrastinating once I realize the social standing of the person I'm supposed to be calling.
- [ ] I believe that at some point in the future I'll have enough experience, education, and poise to call on people who are better than me, but that time is not now.

Is There a Cure?

Social Self-Consciousness is a problem only if up-market buyers are an appropriate and necessary part of your sales strategy. That said, because it's a targeted form, if it's detected early and the proper training is provided, it's a relatively easy form of Call Reluctance to correct. The countermeasures in this book can help alter negative feelings about prospecting to wealthy, prominent, or powerful people.

THE FINAL WORD

"I think that our language, culture, age, fortune, property, and our fame is all a facade. In the end, we're all the same."

— JENOVA CHEN, Video Game Designer

FRIENDSHIELD

When you need a product or service, anything from a good mechanic to a new washing machine, where do you start looking? Chances are, one of your first actions is to ask your friends for recommendations. And if you're in the market for something that a friend can actually provide, whether it's a reliable used car or professional tax advice, you probably turn to them first. After all, given the choice who would you rather do business with — a stranger or someone who (presumably) has your best interest at heart?

Most people readily turn to their friends when they're looking to buy. But salespeople with Friendshield Call Reluctance are emotionally unable to apply the same principle when it comes to selling. They place their friends off-limits when it comes to prospecting, selling, and even asking for the names of other people they might call on. Fearful of upsetting the delicate balance of their relationships, they presume that any attempt to make a sales call on a friend would be met with swift anger and disapproval. So, to prevent conflict and to protect their friendships, salespeople with Friendshield Call Reluctance emotionally shield discussions of business and career interests from their contacts with friends. Sales calls are deemed unacceptable, and asking for referrals is considered a threat to the relationship.

If you struggle with Friendshield Call Reluctance, you reflexively reject your friends as a source of leads, opportunities, and sales. This may or not be based on actual negative reactions you've experienced. You may simply presume your friends would be offended, or feel exploited, if you tried to make a sales presentation to them or asked them for names of other people you might contact. To you it may seem like the safe, protective thing to do. Unfortunately, your competitors may have no such arbitrary rules against selling to their own friends, or yours, and won't hesitate to utilize these networks if you don't.

On the surface, this Call Reluctance type may seem nearly indistinguishable from Famshield Call Reluctance, which erects a similar emotional barrier around relatives. In fact, the two are only moderately related. An analysis of about 63,000 salespeople demonstrated a 39 percent overlap between the two types. That means an individual with Friendshield is not necessarily more likely to have Famshield, or vice versa. In fact, Friendshield Call Reluctance may actually be more functionally related to Role Rejection Call Reluctance. Both types are rooted in the belief that your friends probably hold your sales career in the same low esteem that you do.

Friendshield (known as Separationist in our earlier research) is the ninth most commonly observed type of Call Reluctance. In many industries and professions, it can choke off a potentially rich source of prospects, especially if you're just starting out. After all, your friends should be among the most receptive and amiable audience you'll ever find for your product or service. But if you place an arbitrary gag order on discussing these interests with them, the opportunities can very well die in obscurity.

Here are some of the "soft costs" that can be associated with Friendshield Call Reluctance:

- Difficulty building a client base (due to excluding a significant portion of the prospecting opportunities that are available)
- Struggling with anger or frustration from having to constantly justify not calling on friends
- Needing to compartmentalize relationships with friends to keep business interests completely separate
- Wasting time and energy attempting to "protect" friends from "offensive" selling behavior instead of taking advantage of natural opportunities to advocate and sell

Where Does It Come From?

Friendshield Call Reluctance is learned. It can be passively acquired through exposure to negative stereotypes about selling. Among the "helpful" advice we've found are articles with titles like "Friends Don't Let Friends Sell Them Life Insurance" and "The Danger of Selling to Your Friends and Family." Or it can be picked up from direct contact with friends who had negative experiences with salespeople, sales trainers who have undiagnosed Friendshield issues of their own, or even from respected sales role models who carry the virus, unintentionally spreading it to others. According to reports from securities salespeople, some of the commercial sales training and telemarketing programs used in their industry actually endorse and actively teach Friendshield Call Reluctance.

It's important to note that certain industries or individual companies may have policies in place that prohibit selling to personal friends. In that case, excluding them from your market is an ethical or legal issue, not Call Reluctance. But even in situations that don't allow you to sell directly to your friends, there's no prohibition against asking for the names of other people they know that you can call on. Resisting even that level of prospecting is a sign of an emotional rather than practical barrier to your productivity.

The Friendshield Checklist ☑

If you agree with a number of these statements, you may suffer from Friendshield Call Reluctance:

- ☐ I have friends and acquaintances I could contact about buying my product or service.
- ☐ My friends would probably be a good source of referrals if I asked them.
- ☐ I don't make sales calls on my friends as much as I could or should compared to the opportunities that are available.
- ☐ I would never jeopardize a close personal relationship by treating it like just another sales transaction.
- ☐ A significant number of my personal friends probably don't know exactly what I do for a living.

☐ There are undoubtedly many ways to prospect for new business that are more ethical than exploiting my friendships.

☐ I'm not comfortable giving up the names of my friends to salespeople when they ask for a referral.

Can It Be Cured?

Friendshield Call Reluctance is easy to correct if it's properly detected and the appropriate training procedures are used. The earlier it's discovered, the easier it is to overcome.

THE FINAL WORD

"Lots of people want to ride with you in the limo, but what you want is someone who will take the bus with you when the limo breaks down."

— OPRAH WINFREY

FAMSHIELD

Famshield Call Reluctance is a take on a common trope: The unemancipated child. From *Psycho's* "Norman Bates" to *Mommie Dearest's* "Christina Crawford" to "Luke Skywalker," literature and film abound with conflicted characters who can't get free of a complicated relationship with their parents. For people in sales, the consequences may not be as dramatic as your dad lopping off your hand with a lightsaber. But they still take a toll.

Famshield Call Reluctance targets the ability of salespeople to sell to family members. That includes prospecting, making sales presentations, asking for referrals or even requesting help with networking. When relatives are part of the natural market for a product or service, Famshield creates an emotional blockade against including them in the sales process

You may be talented, articulate, experienced and motivated. But if you suffer from Famshield Call Reluctance, all those attributes crumble when it comes to doing business, or even *discussing* business, with your family. No matter how comfortable you are with prospecting in general, the idea of practicing your skills with the people who know you best stops you in your tracks. Do they even know what you do for a living?

To salespeople who struggle with it, Famshield Call Reluctance is like a time machine to a past they never asked to revisit. Adult-like in most other respects, when they interact with their parents or close relatives, they regress to the perceptions, emotions, and behaviors they experienced as children. Once they enter that dangerous landscape, they defend their emotional paralysis with excuses: Prospecting or asking for referrals among members of my own family just won't work. They'll be offended. They'll feel exploited. They don't know anybody (who knows anybody) who could use my services. They won't take me seriously, these are people who changed my diaper! It's just a waste of their time and mine. In essence, they "shield" their family from their career, and vice versa.

In some industries there are legal and ethical considerations involved in selling to family members (stockbrokerage and real estate all are subject to various regulations and disclosures). We're not suggesting you may be call reluctant because you follow the law. That said, we've yet to find an industry where it's illegal to ask your family if they know anyone who might benefit from hearing about your products or services.

We recommend you think carefully before dismissing friends and family as a potential source of referrals for new business. Back in the 1990s we worked with a company that asked us to remove Famshield and Friendshield (which were then known as Emotionally Unemancipated and Separationist Call Reluctance, respectively) from our Call Reluctance scale reporting. Company executives insisted that family and friend networks, and a salesperson's willingness to utilize them, weren't relevant to their business. But a subsequent pilot study revealed that scores on two particular scales of our assessment were more predictive of a salesperson's success in that organization than any other.

They were Famshield and Friendshield. Salespeople with lower scores sold more, and those with higher scores consistently sold less. Those networks may not have seemed important to the people buying the test, but to the people *taking* it, they meant the difference between success and failure.

There are legitimate reasons why you might not include family members in your selling strategy. If close relatives are genuinely unavailable due to death, distance, or estrangement, it's unlikely that Famshield Call Reluctance, even if present, is significantly limiting the number of contacts you could be initiating. Nonetheless, if you systematically exclude parents, siblings, and other relatives from your prospecting strategy, ask yourself why. Are your reasons based on ethics, lack of available contact, or objective facts (i.e., you know from experience that they resist or disapprove of your efforts)? Or have you simply erected an emotional wall around the very idea of including them?

True story: We teach four-day management training workshops all over the world to help salespeople and sales managers overcome Call Reluctance. At the end of one session in Sweden, co-author Trelitha Bryant was approached by a very tall salesperson. He explained that he had never told his family what he did for a living. Even though Bryant had to crane her neck to look up at this giant of a man, he was telling her how fearful he was. Then he thanked her for the workshop because he said it helped him to better manage his fear. He went on to explain that the night before, he had decided to tell his mother that he was in sales. She listened carefully to him and, to his amazement, responded by giving him three referrals then and there! He told Bryant the workshop had helped to change his life. He spoke as if a huge burden had been lifted off his shoulders.

Famshield is the 12th most commonly observed type of Call Reluctance, suggesting that most salespeople recognize and accept the importance of family members as a natural extension of their target market. But if you don't, you may be missing out on a vital source of leads, opportunities, and closed sales.

Here are a few of the attitudes and beliefs that may accompany Famshield Call Reluctance:

- Business and family should never mix.
- Calling on family members is never appropriate.
- Salespeople who prospect among their own relatives are unprofessional and/or unethical.
- Relatives are incapable of separating family dynamics from a professional relationship.

Where Does It Come From?

Famshield Call Reluctance is entirely learned behavior. The predisposition to it is usually set into motion long before entry into a sales career. Your family dynamics have a lot to do with it. So does the extent to which close relatives expressed negative opinions of salespeople when you were growing up. In your professional life, it can be shaped and encouraged (unintentionally or otherwise) by management, training programs, corporate policies, and stories from peers about their own bad experiences selling to relatives.

The Famshield Checklist ☑

If you agree with a number of these statements, you may suffer from Famshield Call Reluctance:

- ☐ I don't prospect among members of my family or ask them for referrals.
- ☐ I'm not comfortable asking my relatives to introduce me to people in their business or social networks who may be interested in my product or service.
- ☐ Even if they wanted me to, I don't think I could make an effective sales presentation to my family.
- ☐ It really upsets me when salespeople ask me to give them my relatives' contact information so they can try to sell to them.
- ☐ I don't mind if family members try to sell something to *me*, but I just know the situation would be different if the shoe were on the other foot.

Can It Be Cured?

Famshield Call Reluctance is easy to correct once it's been properly detected. The countermeasures in the book can help disassemble the emotional wall between you and this potentially rich source of opportunities.

THE FINAL WORD

"So much of great American drama has been
about a certain kind of dysfunctional family, and maybe
my interests are in the kind of strange dysfunction
that exists even among deeply functional families."

— STEPHEN KARAM, Playwright

REFERRAL AVERSION

Referral Aversion Call Reluctance is unusual among the targeted types in that it may not affect your current sales opportunities. Instead it takes aim at your *next* sale. It emotionally limits your access to prospects you don't even know about yet.

Referrals are names of potential customers you don't know that you get from people you do know. They're a fast, direct route to greater visibility and increased sales. If an existing client or acquaintance entrusts you with someone else's contact info, they're essentially providing a built-in recommendation that the prospect should at least give you a chance. That's an invaluable advantage when you're making that initial contact.

Referrals can be obtained during your sales presentation, after the close, when the order is delivered, and any time afterward. But you have to ask.

If you suffer from Referral Aversion Call Reluctance, asking for those referrals is difficult and distressful. Whether due to lack of experience or a previous bad experience, you probably don't ask for referrals early enough, often enough . . . or at all.

One study showed that 87 percent of satisfied customers are happy to give referrals, while only 7 percent are actually asked.[2] Some unknown portion of those many unasked-for referrals undoubtedly were linked to Call Reluctance. But the larger issue is that the vast majority of potential sales from referrals die on the vine because the request is never made. If you are (or can become) comfortable with asking existing customers for referrals, you open up opportunities for yourself that (almost literally) none of your competitors are pursuing.

Salespeople with Referral Aversion Call Reluctance fear that asking for referrals will threaten a just-closed sale, damage current relationships, or appear grasping and exploitative. They cope by hesitating, putting off the request for referrals as long as they can, or avoiding the situation altogether by never asking. Although the manner of coping may differ, the result is always the same. By failing to follow through with the entire sales process, including asking for referrals, *they default on the bridge to their next sale.*

Relative to other types of Call Reluctance, Referral Aversion is not a particularly common or costly type. That is, unless it happens to you. Conventional wisdom suggests that a good salesperson can turn about 25 percent of initial contacts into closed sales (assuming, of course, those initial contacts are made). On the other hand, 50 percent (or more) of calls to referrals result in sales. What does that difference mean to you in dollars and cents? Is it an amount you can afford to sacrifice to fear?

Here are some of the ways Referral Aversion can sound and feel:

- Distress about asking for referrals that increases as the time draws near, potentially damaging other parts of the sales process.
- Self-protective insistence that providing excellent customer service will prompt clients to volunteer referrals without being asked.
- Belief that the "right time" must present itself

during the sale before the subject of referrals can be brought up.
- (Unsupported) belief that "most" customers feel offended or exploited when asked to provide a referral.

Where Does It Come From?

Referral Aversion is learned. No one is born with it. Sometimes all it takes is one bad experience, an unexpected rude or angry response to a referral request. Interestingly, that client's rude response may itself have been a reaction to one bad experience being badgered for a referral by a pushy, over-aggressive salesperson, creating a vicious cycle of negative feelings about referrals on both sides. In any event, if the original experience was sufficiently intense, it becomes generalized to all referrals and superimposed over future opportunities. Eventually, it feels as if asking for referrals actually *causes* emotional distress. It doesn't. The distress is the result of a false narrative you've allowed yourself to believe.

The Referral Aversion Checklist ☑

If you recognize yourself in several of the following, you may struggle with Referral Aversion Call Reluctance:

☐ My product or service easily lends itself to contacting referrals given by current or past clients.

☐ I don't ask for referrals as often as I could or should because it makes me uncomfortable.

☐ I don't have any problem giving referrals when I've received excellent service, but I don't believe most other people feel the same way.

☐ I don't find it easy to ask for referrals, so I keep a canned script in my head that sounds stiff and unconvincing, even to me.

☐ Sometimes I get too nervous to ask for referrals when the time is right, and then I feel it's too late to go back and ask later.

☐ It's tacky for people I know to approach my clients to ask for referrals.

Can It Be Cured?

Armed with appropriate training aids, Referral Aversion Call Reluctance is easy to prevent, diagnose and correct. The countermeasures in this book can effectively reduce or eliminate negative thoughts about asking for referrals.

THE FINAL WORD

"If you don't ask, you'll never know.
Be an educated risk taker."

— ALIZA LICHT, founder and president
of Leave Your Mark, LLC

TELEPHOBIA

Telephobia Call Reluctance is a highly selective impairment. In an era when people and businesses are almost intimately connected by electronic communication and social media, it centers exclusively around hesitation to use a 20th-century tool: the telephone. Some salespeople with Telephobia claim to have driven 100 miles or more to follow up on dubious leads because they were unable to prospect by phone. A computer salesperson with Telephobia summed it up this way: "The telephone is an annoyance and a hindrance to all mankind. I wish Alexander Graham Bell had never been born." This salesman had recently (reluctantly) participated in a basic telemarketing course. He knew what to say and how to say it when he got on the phone. He didn't know how to do so comfortably.

If you struggle with Telephobia Call Reluctance, you may not have issues with any other forms of prospecting, your discomfort is laser-focused on initiating contact by making phone calls. Interestingly, your discomfort may be further restricted to making calls for the purpose of business development and self-promotion. Calling a friend or ordering a pizza, no problem. But initiating contact with a prospective buyer or client is an emotional non-starter.

Recent research into Telephobia has been colored by a question that's become prevalent in the business world: Is the phone even relevant as a contact initiation tool in the 21st century? It's easy to find statistics that suggest the humble phone call may be going the way of the telegram.

For example, one survey found that among Millennials, making calls was only the fifth most common application they used on their cell phones. On the other hand, in some estimates the "open" rate of a text message is as high as 99 percent. Meanwhile, every year people report less willingness to answer the phone, particularly when Caller ID shows a toll-free or unrecognized number. These statistics don't seem to bode well for telephone prospecting.

But there's another side to the story. We conducted a survey of more than 4,700 sales professionals asking them what they thought was the most effective means of contact. 31 percent indicated that phone calls are the best method, second only to in-person interactions (39 percent) and far above email, text, mailouts and other indirect platforms (15.3 percent). What's more, the results were consistent across all age groups. Immediacy, interactivity, and ability to forge an emotional connection all make the case that the telephone still has a vital role to play in the sales process.

In addition, the phone remains an important tool for closing sales, not just for initiating contact. It's generally acknowledged that a closed sale may require up to five phone calls *after* an initial meeting. Interestingly, a majority of salespeople give up after only one or two follow-ups, effectively sacrificing those sales.

All of this adds up to a straightforward conclusion: If you can't or won't make phone calls because of Telephobia Call Reluctance, you're likely wasting time and effort on alternative strategies that are simply less effective. Whether you're selling a product, working for a political campaign or trying to build a business, reluctance to consistently prospect over the phone is probably costing you.

Telephobia is the 10th most frequently occurring type of Call Reluctance. Statistically, almost 26 percent of all salespeople will experience it. It also has the single largest impact on overall prospecting.

Here are some of the energy-sapping ways Telephobia Call Reluctance takes a toll on prospecting activity:

- Reliance on less effective prospecting methods that don't require using the phone.
- Over-investment in tech-based solutions, like auto-dialers, which aren't inherently bad things. In fact, they can be good things. They become problematic, however, when they're used as a crutch to compensate for a salesperson's inability to call a prospect.
- Lack of phone follow-up to leads generated by other sources.
- Tendency to take long, frequent breaks during scheduled prospecting times.
- An abundance of nervous mannerisms (laughter, stammering, rambling) while on the phone.

Where Does It Come From?

Telephobia is a 100 percent learned behavior. Most cases spring from one or more past events when the use of the telephone became connected to intense feelings of alarm or threat. Perhaps you called someone who, for reasons unrelated to you as a person, angrily hung up. Perhaps you've received bad news by telephone, or grew up with a family member who regarded any phone call as rude and intrusive. Any of these early experiences can sow the seeds of later distress related to the phone.

Telephobia Call Reluctance is sustained by our native ability to mindlessly over generalize negative experiences and then repeat those generalizations as if they were true. A single, long forgotten attempt to use the phone for prospecting purposes is usually enough. Years later, the unpleasant sensations you experienced with that phone call can still be superimposed on all phones you try to use for prospecting purposes.

The Telephobia Checklist ☑

If you agree with a number of these statements, you may struggle with Telephobia Call Reluctance:

- ☐ I don't initiate contact with prospective buyers via telephone as much as I should, given the opportunities that are available.
- ☐ I feel relieved when I successfully avoid making a prospecting phone call.
- ☐ I have to get psyched up to make phone calls, and a single rejection can deflate me.
- ☐ Having to make phone calls in the presence of managers or trainers causes me even more discomfort than I already feel.
- ☐ I've been known to pre-emptively hang up on phone calls I've made before I can be rejected or turned down.

☐ Whenever possible, I try to get other people to make calls on my behalf or to call me so that I don't have to make a cold call.

Can It Be Cured?

Telephobia Call Reluctance is usually easy to diagnose and correct once a serious commitment is made and serious countermeasures are used. If left unmanaged, especially in large organizations, it can promptly expand to epidemic proportions. Left undiagnosed in sales managers, trainers, or senior sales executives, the prognosis is corporate self-destruction.

THE FINAL WORD

"The great dreaded thing every reporter lives with is what you don't know. The source you didn't go to. The phone call you didn't return."

— BOB WOODWARD, Journalist

ONLINE PROSPECTING DISCOMFORT

Online Prospecting Discomfort is just what it sounds like: Emotional discomfort associated with using modern, web-based applications to initiate contact with prospective buyers. This can include hesitation to leverage social media accounts, web conferencing programs and networking sites. These channels are becoming increasingly important to sales and marketing efforts in many industries, and avoiding them can be costly.

In a way, Online Prospecting Discomfort is like reverse Telephobia. Instead of avoiding traditional means of communication (phone calls), salespeople with Online Prospecting Discomfort surrender opportunities to reach certain markets that prefer to do business primarily or exclusively online. It's a highly targeted fear.

To be clear, "new media" selling is simply another tool in your prospecting toolkit. It's not a magic bullet, or a guaranteed path to sales success. To the extent that you're able to prospect by other means, it may not affect your ability to promote your product or service very much. But if your prospective buyers expect to access product videos on YouTube, ask questions on Twitter, or negotiate over a Skype call — and you're invisible on those platforms — you may be putting yourself at a disadvantage compared to your competitors.

Here are a few of the marker behaviors of Online Prospecting Discomfort:

- Reliance on traditional "offline" methods of business development to the exclusion of technology-based approaches

- A limited or inconsistent online presence/identity
- Avoiding or ignoring opportunities to create web-based sales presentations or demonstrations
- Tendency to become easily frustrated when using (or attempting to learn) online prospecting/networking tools
- Stubborn rejection of the value of online prospecting/selling, without making a legitimate effort to test its effectiveness

Unsurprisingly, studies show that this type of Call Reluctance is much more prevalent among salespeople "of a certain age." Seasoned veterans, no matter their skill and experience level, have spent a relatively small percentage of their lives immersed in technology compared to younger colleagues. While some embrace the new frontier of online selling, others resist the rapid changes taking place in their profession. They may feel frustrated and powerless when faced with new platforms, especially if they feel they have no choice but to adopt them. Researchers have dubbed these negative feelings "technostress."

Interestingly, our research shows that when it comes to Online Prospecting Discomfort, there's no defined cut-off age that separates those who are susceptible to it and those who aren't. When salespeople are grouped according to age, every decade (beginning with the twenty-somethings) shows less discomfort with online prospecting than the decade just before it. In other words, while salespeople in their 60s tend to have higher

Online Prospecting Discomfort scores than those in their 50s, the fifty-somethings in turn have higher scores than those in their 40s, and so on. It appears that as technology rapidly develops, even the wunderkind of the previous decade seem to reach a point when the latest generation of tech begins to generate more distress.

Where Does It Come From?

Our research into Online Prospecting Discomfort is still in its formative stages. Right now it appears to be mainly a training issue, significantly influenced by generational factors. The shift to online prospecting and selling methods is ongoing and evolving at a seemingly exponential rate. The rapid rate of change is in itself enough to trigger Online Prospecting Discomfort in some. For others, a lack of familiarity with technology and social media in general is likely behind their inability to comfortably exploit the new opportunities that are available. For still others, news stories about hacking scandals and concern for maintaining traditional notions of privacy may lead to hesitation to embrace online prospecting.

We think it's important to note that, like all forms of Call Reluctance, Online Prospecting Discomfort is distinguished by avoidance based primarily on emotional, rather than rational, factors. For example, we worked with a gentleman who happened to be a consultant that trains salespeople. He adamantly insisted to us that "new media" prospecting was *completely* irrelevant for him. His clients preferred face-to-face or telephone contact. He insisted that reaching out to prospective new customers via mutual connections on LinkedIn *absolutely* would not work. When we asked, "Have you tried it?" his response was, "No." What's more, it was clear he didn't plan to try it.

The Online Prospecting Checklist ☑

If you agree with a number of these statements, you may struggle with Online Prospecting Call Reluctance:

- ☐ I consider myself a traditionalist when it comes to prospecting and selling techniques.
- ☐ If I can't get a prospect to buy based on my own abilities, a blog or a tweet isn't going to help.
- ☐ I get overwhelmed by new technology sometimes.
- ☐ When I see other people constantly going online, I can't help but wonder if they're actually working or just wasting time.
- ☐ I wouldn't know where to begin to establish an online presence.

Can It Be Cured?

The most important factor in "curing" this form of Call Reluctance may be whether the salesperson wants to be cured. Employing traditional forms of prospecting over "new media" contacts may be a preference too deeply ingrained to change in some salespeople. But for those who are willing to address their discomfort, Online Prospecting Discomfort seems to respond favorably to training. Studies have shown that when companies commit to smoothly integrating new technologies into their selling strategy, and when adequate technical and organizational support is provided to salespeople, the incidence of technostress in general and

Online Prospecting Discomfort in particular decreases.

THE FINAL WORD

"The mechanical loom and the calculator have shown us that technology is both disruptive and filled with opportunities. But it would be hard to find a decent argument that we would have been better off without these inventions."

— OREN ETZIONI, CEO, Allen Institute
for Artificial Intelligence

COMPLEX SALES

Complex Sales Call Reluctance occurs in salespeople who experience discomfort with multi-layered, multi-contact selling environments. Instead of inhibiting their ability to initiate a single contact, it can strike over and over during the course of a sale, damaging (or destroying) the desired outcome from multiple angles.

Complex sales, or enterprise sales, represent a relatively new but rapidly expanding approach to the relationship between buyers and sellers. In a highly competitive market, where multiple companies may offer similar products and services, some buyers have implemented sophisticated procurement processes to get the most out of their vendor relationships. They expect more than a simple "pitch." They're looking for a partner who under-stands their business and suggests multi-dimensional solutions. For vendors, that has led to the recognition that the traditional sales approach emphasizing price and features often puts them at a disadvantage. To set themselves apart in a crowded field, sales organizations have increasingly adopted a solution-based selling model involving detailed proposals and pairing product offer-ings with unique insights and industry expertise.

Building a relationship based on partnering rather than simply purchasing generally requires buy-in from multiple levels of the client company. It also requires coordination among different functional areas that may include engineering, logistics, and marketing as well as sales. For that reason, enterprise selling typically involves a longer sales cycle in which teams from both the buying side and the selling side interact repeatedly to tailor a solution or suite of products. In this environment, Complex Sales Call Reluctance manifests itself as hesitation to make the number of contacts required, with the number of players required, to bring the sale to a successful conclusion.

Not all products and services lend themselves to a complex sales process, of course. Complex Sales Call Reluctance doesn't necessarily affect traditional, "single touch" prospecting and selling (although it may impede your ability to comfortably follow up on those initial contacts later). But if your organization is moving to an enterprise sales model, Complex Sales Call Reluctance may place you on the wrong side of what authors and researchers Matthew Dixon and Brent Adamson call "a widening talent gap" between traditional transaction-based selling and the opportunities of this type of selling.

Here are some of the unproductive attitudes and behaviors associated with this type:

- Uncomfortable contacting senior-level executives or decision-makers (similar to Social Self-Consciousness but for different reasons)
- Prefers transactional sales with a linear structure and a short timeframe
- May hesitate to make necessary, repeated contacts with the buyer as part of negotiations
- May confuse low-pressure rapport building with the assertive skillset required of complex sales.
- Prefers selling alone instead of as part of a coordinated team effort

Where Does It Come From?

The unique nature of enterprise selling creates a fertile environment for various negative thoughts to take root and grow into contact-inhibiting behaviors. Complex Sales Call Reluctance, therefore, may "borrow" the behavioral signatures of multiple other Call Reluctance types. This type of selling requires several different kinds of "touches," creating multiple portals where fear can intrude upon the sales process. Yielder tendencies may emerge in the form of hesitation to persistently follow up and assertively negotiate throughout the sale. Stage Fright may rear its head if the deal requires making boardroom presentations, while Social Self-Consciousness can come into play when high-level decision-makers must be consulted. Inhibiting necessary goal-supporting behaviors at various points in the sales process, Complex Sales Call Reluctance can make the entire process feel emotionally threatening and out-of-bounds.

As a highly situational form of Call Reluctance, Complex Sales takes root when salespeople are exposed to this type of selling without proper support from managers, trainers, and other people in the organization tasked with shifting corporate culture to an enterprise selling mindset. If you're already predisposed to emotional discomfort with the individual contact initiation behaviors that make up complex sales, then you're likely to struggle when confronted with them all in a concentrated sales setting.

The Complex Sales Checklist ☑

If you agree with several of these statements, you may suffer from Complex Sales Call Reluctance:

- ☐ I feel as if I'm watching other people in my organization put together big sales while I'm observing from the sidelines.
- ☐ I don't understand why I can't just sell the way I've always done it, without making it a big production.
- ☐ I feel as if I'm much more effective making a deal when I'm one-on-one and don't have to get the buy-in of a room full of people.
- ☐ I miss the days when all it took to make a sale was a good product and good rapport with the customer.
- ☐ It's hard to stay enthusiastic about a sale when I have to keep following up for weeks at a time.
- ☐ It's frustrating having to rely on other people to get my job done.

Can It Be Cured?

Successfully introducing an enterprise selling model in an organization requires commitment and support from the highest level managers to the rank and file salespeople. With proper training and orientation, Complex Sales Call Reluctance can probably be reduced or eliminated.

THE FINAL WORD

"It's hard to beat a person who never gives up."

— BABE RUTH, American Baseball Player

SALES EXTENSIONS

Sales Extensions Call Reluctance occurs when opportunities to make additional sales to existing customers are neglected or avoided due to discomfort. Similar to Referral Aversion and Close Reluctance, Sales Extensions doesn't typically affect the initiation phase of the sales process. Instead, hesitation occurs at the end of the sale, when *influencing* gives way to *avoiding*. Specifically, hesitation occurs when the opportunity arises to suggest product or service "add-ons." Apprehensive about offending customers or risking previous rapport by attempting to cross-sell, on-sell, or up-sell, these salespeople fail to capitalize on a natural bridge to additional sales.

If you work in a selling environment where promoting product upgrades, accessories, or warranties is a natural and expected part of the sales process, Sales Extensions Call Reluctance may significantly affect your ability to excel.

Sales Extensions Call Reluctance can take three forms. One or more of these sub-types may be negatively affecting your selling activity.

Cross-Selling: Discomfort centers around attempting to persuade an existing client to purchase an additional product or service that your company offers, which may be different from and unrelated to what the client has purchased before.

Example: "If you're pleased with the business cards we designed for you, you may also want to speak to someone in our web design division who can help you add functionality to your company website. I'd be happy to set up a meeting."

Up-Selling: Discomfort centers around ethically attempting to sell a more expensive or upgraded product to an existing client.

Example: "I'm happy to sell you the $200 mobile phone you're inquiring about. But you did say you want a really great quality camera. You may not be happy with the resolution of the pictures from the phone you're looking at. The $700 one over here has a much better camera . . . "

On-Selling: Discomfort centers around attempting to sell product/service accessories that augment the original purchase (warranties, service contracts, etc.)

Example: "For an extra $15, we can add the Protection Package, which means we'll repair or replace your widget if anything goes wrong with it within the first year. Would you be interested in adding that today?"

Here are some marker behaviors of Sales Extensions Call Reluctance:

- Selling fewer add-ons (and making fewer attempts to sell them) compared to your peers.
- Habitually failing to take advantage of opportunities to offer logical companion products/services to clients.
- Ignoring or rebuffing colleagues who express interest in approaching your clients with additional or upgraded products.
- Insisting to management that customers don't want or need product/service upgrades, *without actually having asked them.*

Where Does It Come From?

Sales Extensions Call Reluctance is a learned avoidance behavior. Its source is frequently one or more past experiences with customers who reacted negatively to your up-selling efforts. It can also sprout from managers or trainers who struggle with the same discomfort and pass it on to you by subtly discouraging this type of behavior.

One of the more spectacular stories we've heard about the origins of this kind of fear came from a client's personal experience. He was a young bank teller back in the day when banks first hit on the idea that their tellers should also cross-sell financial services. One day, he was processing a customer's withdrawal and, as he'd been trained to do, asked if the customer would like to speak with an in-house investment advisor.

The customer responded by pulling a gun on him. It was a bank robbery, an actual stick-up! From that moment on, our client's brain "stapled" that kind of prospecting to a real-life, very threatening situation. It stayed that way for decades, preventing him from comfortably pursuing those opportunities, until we were able to help him detach the two.

The Sales Extensions Checklist ☑

If you agree with several of these statements, you may struggle with Sales Extensions Call Reluctance:

☐ I probably don't attempt to take advantage of add-on sales opportunities as often as I could or should.

☐ I hesitate to push alternative or additional products on my customers that they haven't asked about.

☐ My clients would be angry or offended if I exploited our relationship by allowing my colleagues to try to sell them additional products.

☐ I have difficulty finding ways to on-sell without sounding forced or predatory.

☐ I'd rather settle for a smaller commission than risk offending people.

☐ Even when a natural opportunity exists to make an add-on sale, sometimes I feel too uncomfortable to try.

Can It Be Cured?

As a learned and highly targeted form of Call Reluctance, the outlook for overcoming anxiety connected to sales extensions is very positive.

THE FINAL WORD:

"Often when you think you're at the end of something, you're at the beginning of something else."

— FRED ROGERS (1920–2003), Author and TV Icon

CLOSE RELUCTANCE

For many years, Close Reluctance (aka "Arranging Payment Reluctance" in some of our recent work) was considered a marker behavior of Yielder Call Reluctance. Hesitation to close a sale is a frequent byproduct of the Yielder's overall discomfort with assertive behavior and fear of being seen as pushy by customers. Only in recent years have we been able to isolate the specific act of naming a price and closing a deal as a distinct form of Call Reluctance, one that is related to but far more focused on this specific part of the sales process than the more diffused Yielder.

Our research historically has focused on the importance of comfortably and consistently prospecting for new business. Without prospective customers in the pipeline, no selling can occur. But if initiating contact is the opening shot in the sales process, closing the sale is the critical target. Sales training expert Brian Tracy wrote about the "core requirement" of *obtaining commitment*: "[The] ability to . . . obtain commitment to take action is the endgame of selling. If you do everything well except for this, you will still fail."

Unlike other forms of Call Reluctance, Close Reluctance doesn't negatively affect prospecting at all. Rather than stifling the *initiation* part of the sales process, it takes a toll on *influencing* — getting the client to buy, agree, or otherwise commit to closing a deal. If you suffer from Close Reluctance, the emotional discomfort comes at the back end of the sale, when the time comes to discuss price, payment and delivery. You may stumble and stammer, squandering the energy and enthusiasm you've built up in your prospect while hoping that they'll take a hint and volunteer to close the sale for you. Unfortunately, they're just as likely to become confused when no request to buy is forthcoming, get bored waiting for you to do your job, and lose interest.

Here's what Close Reluctance looks like in the selling environment:

- Hesitation to communicate cost and payment options or ask the prospect to sign an agreement at the end of the sales presentation
- Spending a disproportionate amount of time building rapport with the prospect
- Drawing out the sales presentation with frequent lunches, meetings, and follow ups
- Tendency to miss or ignore "buying signs" that would trigger the closing portion of the sale
- Fear of alienating or offending clients by bringing up cost

Where Does It Come From?

Close Reluctance, like its cousin Yielder Call Reluctance, frequently is learned from managers and trainers who over-emphasize "soft-selling" approaches. In a misguided (and increasingly discredited) attempt to position inter-personal relationships as *the main reason* people buy, these approaches often instill the idea that assertive selling is obnoxious and pushy. If you internalize this idea, you may come to believe that not only is "obtaining commitment" not foundational to sales, it's actually a bad thing. Too much of your energy goes into creating conditions favorable to making a sale . . . and not enough into actually asking the customer to buy.

We've found that professional "relationship builders" with Yielder tendencies are particularly susceptible to discomfort when it's time to move the relationship from social interaction to a business transaction. Not long ago, a pharmaceutical company sent participants to our management training workshop because of a particular, costly problem. Their reps routinely built good relationships with doctors — playing golf, bringing in lunch, and generally creating goodwill. But the doctors, although they seemingly enjoyed and encouraged the relationships, were writing prescriptions for their competitors' drugs instead. Why? Simple: While our client was plying the physicians with expensive, feel-good perks, the competitors' sales reps were *actually asking the doctors to write prescriptions for their drugs*. Rapport is important, but there's no substitute for closing.

The Close Reluctance Checklist ☑

If you agree with several of these statements, you may suffer from Close Reluctance:

- ☐ My sales numbers don't reflect the amount of prospecting and selling I actually do.
- ☐ I usually don't have much trouble engaging prospects, but I still struggle to get them to buy.
- ☐ I believe people get personally offended when a

salesperson tries to name a price before proving his worth and value to them.

- ☐ Sometimes I find myself using psychological gimmicks (like silence or extended eye contact) to try to compel the customer to buy.
- ☐ My sales presentations tend to ramble as I get more nervous about having to name the price.
- ☐ If I've built a rapport with a prospect, I don't want to ruin it by pushing for a decision or asking for payment.
- ☐ If my prospect likes me, I don't have to ask for their business. They'll let me know when they're ready to buy from me.

Can It Be Cured?

Fortunately, Close Reluctance is fairly easy to eliminate in a motivated, goal-directed salesperson. The counter-measures in this book can help redirect your energy from coping to closing sales.

THE FINAL WORD

"Sales are contingent upon the attitude of the salesman, not the attitude of the prospect."

— WILLIAM CLEMENT STONE, Businessman,
Philanthropist and Author

CALL RELUCTANCE CALLING CARDS BY INDUSTRY

Fear is personal. Patterns of escape and avoidance can be as individual as fingerprints. Yours may differ from those of your colleagues, your managers, your significant others. That's why we've developed assessment tools to help pinpoint your most costly prospecting habits.

Still, it can be helpful to compare the types of Call Reluctance that are most prevalent in various settings. Here is the most financially limiting Call Reluctance variant in 17 types of sales based on our research.

Advertising	Over Preparer
Agriculture Equipment Sales	Close Reluctance
Banking	Yielder
Construction	Yielder
Education	Over Preparer
Financial Services	Yielder
Food & Beverage	Over Preparer
Healthcare/Medical	Yielder
Hospitality/Leisure	Yielder
HR/Recruiting	Close Reluctance
Industrial Services & Supplies	Close Reluctance
Insurance Agents & Brokers	Telephobia
Real Estate	Stage Fright
Renewable Energy	Oppositional Reflex
Retail Sales	Yielder
Software/Tech Sales	Over Preparer
Training/Consulting	Yielder

5

The Countermeasures

ongratulations on making it this far. Now that you know how your fears may be sapping your energy and straining your wallet, we hope you're asking yourself, "What's next?"

If you're seeing this because you randomly flipped or scrolled to this page without reading what came before it: We commend your willingness to dive into the swimming pool blindfolded. You don't even know if it has water in it! Water is probably overrated anyway. We invite you to take off the blindfold so you can see what you're getting into. Start reading on page 1. We'll be waiting to congratulate you when you get here.

While we hope you've enjoyed your journey to this point, be aware that learning about Call Reluctance is unlikely to magically control it. Busting barriers to prospecting and self-promotion requires action on your part. To be relentless you have to be resolute, and the longer you've struggled, the more determined you'll need to be. The remainder of this book is dedicated to teaching you how to apply proven countermeasures to help you reduce your distress and increase your prospecting activity.

The techniques presented here aren't gimmicks or mind tricks. They're based on solid psychological principles, although we've stripped away much of the psychological jargon. Our focus here is on practical application rather than the complexities of brain wiring. That information is readily available in all of its jargon-y glory if you want the full backstory. We're just not covering it in detail here. (Feel free to ask us, but be forewarned: We have Over-Preparer tendencies. We like to explain things. A lot.)

We divide Call Reluctance countermeasures into two types: Word-based and Mechanical. Word-based procedures are designed to tap into your faculties for cognitive reasoning and self-persuasion. As the name suggests, they rely on words to help you defuse and dispel your fears. They also require that you *understand* and *agree with* the principles behind them, at least to some degree, in order to work. Mechanical procedures, on the other hand, aren't based on logic, reasoning, or verbal comprehension. They bypass cognitive functions and work on a physiological level to combat negative reactions to prospecting. You don't have to agree or understand. You just have to follow instructions.

Which countermeasures work for you will depend largely on your personality predispositions, as well as the specific type(s) of Call Reluctance you want to correct. We've included both word-based and mechanical procedures in the following chapters.

Variations of the countermeasures have appeared in popular media and self-help programs, so you're probably superficially familiar with them. "Snap myself with a rubber band? I read about that on HuffPost!" Even so, we encourage you to pay close attention in order to understand a) the appropriate way to apply them (which most media outlets omit or get wrong) and b) how to use them specifically to counteract Call Reluctance.

Changing unproductive behaviors is a process, and applying the countermeasures is one part of that process. You've already begun by reading to this point. Now let's take a look at the other pieces of the puzzle.

There are four steps to overcoming Call Reluctance. They're simple, but they're not necessarily easy. Some people may never allow themselves to successfully navigate them. Others may not be ready to start today. That's OK. At some point the combination of energy-sapping fear and wallet-punishing missed opportunities will prod them to begin the journey (if it hasn't already derailed their career). Whether it happens next week or next year, the steps remain the same.

They are:

Admit. Before you can change your behavior, you need to admit to yourself that you struggle with Call Reluctance and that it's keeping you from earning what you're worth. That can be difficult, but it's doable. If you can't bring yourself to admit it, are you willing to concede that it's possible? Try it; it may be the nudge you need to get to the next step.

Diagnose. To understand exactly what you're up against, you should diagnose the specific type or types of Call Reluctance currently limiting you. Use the rating scales in Chapter 2 or seek out the assessments we've created to accurately detect and define the problem. Ask your friends, colleagues, and managers for insights into your behavior that may not be obvious to you. They can help you pinpoint your fears. But resist the urge to get too deep into the weeds about where your Call Reluctance issues came from. It may be interesting, but it's not necessary to correct the problem. Stubbornly insisting that you understand before taking action can actually become just another excuse to avoid addressing your career-limiting attitudes. And remember that the countermeasures are designed to address authentic Call Reluctance. If your explorations lead you to the conclusion that you're dealing with impostor issues instead (see Chapter 3), they won't help you right now.

Match. Choose which Call Reluctance type(s) you're going to tackle and match them to the countermeasures that follow. Study the procedures carefully and do exactly what they say. Don't argue with them and don't modify or skip steps that make you feel uncomfortable. That's important. Finally, don't confuse a natural desire to understand *how* the countermeasures work with your real objective: To increase your prospecting activity.

Finally, **follow up**. Actually make calls. Increasing your self-awareness may make you feel better, but it's not the goal. Don't convince yourself that a change in your outlook is the same thing as a measurable increase in the number of contacts you initiate. A bad attitude in a top producer isn't optimal, but it's tolerable. A good attitude in a non-producer may be endearing, but it can be fatal to your career.

We're going to introduce you to three powerful prescriptions to treat your Call Reluctance symptoms. They are:

Thought Realignment (Word-Based)
Thought Zapping (Mechanical)
Sensory Injection (Mechanical)

These techniques are designed to challenge counterproductive feelings you have about prospecting and recapture motivation that you currently squander on coping with your fears. Some touted "cures" for Call Reluctance simply encourage you to slap a new label on your feelings and pretend you believe it — the emotional equivalent of telling yourself how delicious the ketchup is while your tongue is aflame from being doused with habanero sauce. These techniques are designed to attack your fears at the "content" level — actually addressing what's inside the bottle, as it were.

Thought Realignment, Sensory Injection, and Thought Zapping occupy a small corner of the universe of available techniques. Assuming that almost every possible approach will work for *someone*, there are probably hundreds of "cures" for Call Reluctance. Earlier versions of Dudley and Goodson's work outlined six, plus a number of supplemental techniques. We've streamlined our selection to these three. Why? Because we know they're effective. We know they work for many people. And we know they're helpful for most forms of Call Reluctance.

Be aware that Call Reluctance is all about self-protection. Your fears may not surrender without a fight. They may try to convince you, by means of internal dialogue and reflexive denials, that Call Reluctance isn't *that* big a deal, that your coping behaviors aren't costing you very much, even that you don't need to prospect and self-promote to be successful. Don't listen. Don't give up. And don't allow such negative self-talk to continue to take money out of your pocket.

At the end of the day, the best technique for overcoming Call Reluctance is the one that works for you. We won't be insulted if, after reading about the procedures we recommend, you don't use them. But we do encourage you to read about them first, before searching for something different. You've already come this far. What have you got to lose by learning a little more?

If you're ready, let's begin.

THOUGHT REALIGNMENT

Thought Realignment is a special adaptation of a self-talk technique introduced by ancient philosophers, popularized in our time by psychologists Aaron Beck and Albert Ellis, and sensationalized as a modern breakthrough. It's not. The technique, and the philosophical basis from which it grew, is not new. It has a long and distinguished heritage. It asserts that most, if not all, of our distressful feelings are caused by the view we take of things and situations in life, *not* the things and situations themselves.

As a word-based prescription, Thought Realignment calls for a level of self-reflection and intellectual understanding to be successful. Not everyone is inclined to such self-examination. Some salespeople prefer a more down-to-earth, action-oriented approach. Yet in our experience, those who do embrace Thought Realignment tend to be die-hard fans. So although it may take a little more patience than other countermeasures, approached with discipline and an open mind it can produce remarkable changes in attitude and behavior.

Over the years we've come to believe that Thought Realignment works best 1) to prevent Call Reluctance or 2) to act as a "booster shot" after you've addressed Call Reluctance with other countermeasures.

We recommend you read this chapter even if you tend to prefer more action-oriented approaches. It includes a wealth of detail and insight into how your brain processes the sensory input that eventually gets transformed into career-limiting fears. It's interesting and explains some of the mechanisms that make other countermeasures

(Thought Zapping and Sensory Injection) effective. And if you want to try your hand at a more classical approach to managing Call Reluctance, Thought Realignment may be just what you're looking for.

Overview

To quote the Roman philosopher Marcus Aurelius, "If you are pained by an external thing, it is not the thing that disturbs you, but your own judgment about it." In other words, there's nothing in the world as scary as the things we convince ourselves we have to be scared of.

Thought Realignment is based on the principle that what you *say* to yourself about prospecting has a powerful impact on what you *feel* when you prospect. And what you *feel* when you prospect, has a powerful impact on what you *do* about prospecting — before, during, and after making calls.

This countermeasure will teach you to *identify* counter-productive messages hidden in the way you describe prospecting to yourself. Then you'll learn to *control* negative feelings that interfere with prospecting by changing how you describe what prospecting means to you. Finally, you'll *apply* what you've learned by purposefully placing yourself into emotionally difficult prospecting situations while you practice self-management skills that support your career goals.

Four simple steps, but not necessarily easy. Let's break them down.

Step One: Identify the Self-Propaganda Channel

Every day you're exposed to massive amounts of sensory data. And every day you assign meanings to the people, places, things, and situations you perceive. As a human being, when you receive a packet of information from Sensory Central Control, you respond much the same way a computer would: You begin to process it. But unlike a computer, your mind doesn't necessarily proceed in an objective, linear order. The human programming language is less like Java and more like Half-Caf Double-Pump Skinny Caramel Frapp. It's idiosyncratic and subjective. It directs all incoming sensory traffic to a mental gauntlet consisting of a series of perceptual filters. Based on the outcome, you begin the process of deciding 1) what you feel and 2) how much you feel it.

One of the filters waiting to process incoming traffic is *past experience*. It compares incoming information with prior records on file in your memory. The results are the product of your unique experiences. For example, if you and a friend are driving by your old high school, you may enjoy warm recollections of favorite teachers and football games on crisp autumn evenings. But if your friend's high school experience was marked by loneliness or bullying, she will likely experience a very different emotional reaction. If you were to compare memories based on your individual experiences, you might wonder if you had both attended the same school.

Present needs is another filter, which tilts our perceptions toward our immediate physical or emotional requirements. You've probably felt its influence at the grocery store. Have you ever shopped on an empty stomach? How is it different from shopping when you've just eaten a big meal? When you're already hungry, you may instinctively stock up on *everything* and give in to impulses you might otherwise resist if you were feeling full. That's your present needs filter in action.

The last filter consists of your *values*. This one evaluates incoming traffic by comparing it with what you consider to be right and wrong, good and bad. For example, if someone offered you a glass of brandy, you might consider it a kindly warm up for a cold winter's night. But how would you respond if you strongly believe that alcohol consumption is inherently evil and spiritually corrupting?

Your filters exert their influence through *mind chatter*, the ongoing process of describing the world to yourself. Whether you're aware of it or not, you continuously carry on an internal monologue about what you think you see and hear. Because this monologue is a byproduct of your filters, its appraisal of any given situation is highly subjective. Sometimes your inner voice distorts the truth. Sometimes, it flat-out lies.

We call these distortions *mindbenders*. They can cause you to think, feel, and ultimately act in counter-productive ways based on what you tell yourself is happening. When prospecting, they can interfere with your ability to comfortably initiate contacts. Here are some examples.

Mindbender	Your Monologue
Mind-reading: Believing you know what people are "really" thinking.	"This guy thinks I'm wasting his time, I can see it in his eyes. No point trying to sell him anything."
Blaming: Holding people, places, and situations responsible for your behavior.	"The economy is tanking. How am I supposed to sell anything in this market?"
Ruling: Imposing rigid standards or rules on yourself and others	"I can't start making calls until I know I can answer every conceivable question I might be asked."
Weighing: Believing you can impose balance and fairness on your relationships with others	"I buy her kid's band candy every year, but she won't come to one of my seminars? That's so wrong!"
Deferring: Putting off enjoyment for some future time when everything is perfect	"I can't feel proud of myself until I've outsold everyone else in the company. Until then, every day is a bitter struggle."
Selecting: Seeing only one aspect of a person or situation and ignoring all others	"Oh great, this guy has a PhD? There goes any chance I have of making a deal with him."
Dooming: Seeing only terrible, worst-case scenarios	"This audience is going to tear me apart. I'm going to be a total bust."
Affecting: Judging a person or situation based solely on how you feel at the moment	"I'm so angry over how that meeting went. I'll never call on anyone at that company again!"
Informing: Insisting you're always right, even in the face of contradictory evidence.	"I know in my gut that this is the best way to close a deal. Why should I listen to a bunch of eggheads with statistics?"

Relying: Believing that the only person you can ever depend on is yourself.	"My manager only cares about her own numbers. I'll do things my way or not all."
Charming: Believing that others will never act in your interest unless you charm and manipulate them.	"I'll send my client another bottle of that fancy wine before my next call. Then they'll be putty in my hands."
Name-Calling: Labeling or stereotyping people based on a single observation or incident.	"Looks like I need to call on old Snobby Joe with his fancy suits. Time to listen to some more boring fraternity stories."
Defaulting: Feeling helpless because you believe others control what you can and can't do.	"My boss is just going to shoot down this idea, like he shoots down everything else. No wonder I can't get anything done."
Overgeneralizing: Forcing big conclusions from small observations	"Trying to grow a business through social media is futile. Last week three people told me they don't even have a Twitter!"
Personalizing: Believing everything that happens is related significantly to you	"My client just told me they're not accepting new bids. I must have really offended them with the last one I sent."
Controlling: Assuming you have power and control and are responsible for everything and everyone	"ABC Co. just signed a new contract with a different supplier? Good luck with that. They'll come crawling back when they see they can't grow without me."
Polarizing: Seeing everything that happens in either/or extremes	"If I don't hit my numbers this month, I'm done. I may as well move into a homeless shelter."

Mindbenders are wily. They may appear on the surface to be encouraging and self-motivating. Indeed, they may have their basis in positive thoughts, such as "I want my clients to approve of the job I'm doing." Or, "Preparation gives me an important edge over my competitors." But somewhere along the way, your emotional filters twisted and distorted the goal-supportive content of those thoughts. Now those emotionally charged messages have morphed into warnings, alarms, and ultimatums.

Uncritically accepting your negative mind chatter can restrict or even shut down your ability to prospect and self-promote. For example, if you *require* approval and support from every client interaction, what will you do after a rejection? If you allow yourself to believe that you *can't* prospect without 100 percent complete information, then how can you possibly make a call knowing that you haven't yet memorized the price sheet that came out yesterday?

If you're motivated and goal-directed, you may be able to prospect even if your mind chatter contains negative messages like these. But it takes a lot of energy. One workshop participant, who had been successful in his sales career, confessed, "What nobody ever knew was the horrifying things I was telling myself about prospecting from the beginning. Things I never realized, like if I don't get more appointments than anybody else tonight, I won't be the best, and if I'm not the best, then I'm a failure, and if I'm a failure, then I can't provide for my family, and if I don't provide for my family, people will ridicule me, and if people ridiculed me, I would just die."

This salesperson also pointed out two things about his struggle with Call Reluctance to others who were struggling. First, the things he was telling himself weren't true. Second, they had absolutely nothing to do with prospecting. His distress was the direct result of daily doses of self-inflicted verbal poison. But no matter how reckless his self-statements might have been, he accepted them as true at the time. He then acted as if they were true by always being alert to fictional prospecting dangers and being prepared to do battle with the evil Mr. Prospect. Since coping took energy away from meaningful performance, and Mr. Prospect was never the problem in the first place, the real problem got worse, not better. After awhile, he found himself lost in the middle of his career and almost out of gas.

The goal of Thought Realignment is to challenge the mindbenders that poison your thoughts about prospecting and replace them with more supportive, objective thoughts. To challenge them, you first have to be aware of them when they occur. Let's start by learning to tune in to your personal Self-Propaganda Channel.

Step Two: Slow Down and Listen In

The first step in identifying your own verbal poison is to slow it down. The insults and dire warnings you hurl at yourself only need an instant to do their work, and they're stealthy. To bring them out into the open and hear them clearly, it's helpful to slow down your internal monologue. We recommend a simple procedure called "thought deceleration."

Here's how it works. First, just talk to yourself. Don't

talk out loud. Talk the way you normally do when you talk to yourself. Then listen. Notice how your inner voice sounds: How loud is it? What is the tone like? How would other people describe it if they could hear it? If you have trouble hearing your voice, just pretend you hear it and answer the questions. Perhaps when you read you subvocalize (actually say the words to yourself as you read). If so, then use your reading voice.

Next, continue to talk to yourself, but deliberately lower your voice one octave. Imagine your voice is coming from deep down inside your chest. Again, if you have trouble, just pretend to lower your voice. Three things should now happen. The pace of your self-talk automatically slows down when you lower your voice. Your imaginary voice pronounces things more clearly. And it becomes easier to hear the words and phrases and see the mental pictures you associate with them.

Here's a third, optional step. Whenever you thought decelerate, lightly bite your tongue and then say out loud: "This is my thought deceleration cue. Whenever and wherever I do this I will immediately slow down the pace of my self-talk."

If you practice thought deceleration for five minutes, three times a day for three days, something interesting will happen. By lightly biting your tongue, you'll start speaking to yourself in a slower, clearer, more manageable pace. Slowing down enough to take a census of the messages bouncing around inside your head is the first step to cleaning house. Try it.

Once you've slowed things down, you can start listening for content. Unless you're the Most Interesting Man (or Woman) in the World, most of what you hear will be pretty mundane. For our purposes, you can safely ignore it. But the next time you're prospecting (or are about to prospect), tune in to your self-chatter and pay attention. Chances are you'll soon hear your Self-Propaganda Channel broadcasting career-busting messages at full strength. Listen closely. These are the mind-gremlins that lurk beneath the surface of your Call Reluctance.

Each of the Call Reluctance types produces a recognizable mind chatter theme. You may not hear any of them word for word in your own thoughts. But as you learn to listen to yourself, one or more of these themes may come into focus. Do any of these seem familiar?

Yielder: "I must never intrude or impose upon other people, or they'll disapprove of me, and I would be crushed."

Over-Preparer: "I always have to be perfectly prepared before I contact a prospective client, or else they'll think I don't know what I'm talking about. I can't handle that."

Close Reluctance: "I can't risk offending customers by talking about money and payment. I'll lose all the rapport I've built up. I'll just keep talking until they bring it up first."

Complex Sales: "It's awful having to rely on other people to do my job. They never do what they're supposed to do when they're supposed to do it."

Stage Fright: "My presentation has to be dazzling and perfect so that my audience won't dismiss me as incompetent. I'd die up there if I mess up."

Online Prospecting Discomfort: "If I don't make a flawless impression on social media, my prospects will think I'm inept and out of touch. I don't know what I'd do if that happened."

Hyper-Pro: "If I don't appear distinguished and professional in everything I do, people won't respect me. That's about the worst thing I can imagine."

Role Rejection: "All the people I care about must be terribly disappointed that I didn't choose a 'real' career instead of sales. I must pretend to be something better so others will respect me and not judge me."

Friendshield: "I couldn't stand it if my friends ever thought I was exploiting our relationship by trying to sell to them. I must avoid ever discussing business with them."

Telephobia: "People hate to be called on the phone, especially by a salesperson. I can't deal with the rejection coming over the line. I'd better avoid making this call."

Sales Extensions: "Customers just want to make their purchase and be done. They hate pushy salespeople trying to get them to spend more on other things. I need to keep quiet so they don't get annoyed with me."

Famshield: "Mixing business with family is always a bad idea. My relatives would be annoyed, or worse, they wouldn't take me seriously. I have to avoid even the appearance of promoting my business to them."

Social Self-Consciousness: "Wealthy, educated, powerful people are all better than me. They're out of my league, and I shouldn't even attempt to step out of line by trying to sell to them."

Oppositional Reflex: "I couldn't stand ever being hurt or disappointed again, so I must always appear imposing and strong, and make the first strike to avoid looking vulnerable to anyone."

Referral Aversion: "Asking for referrals is an abuse of my client's trust. Buyers are always offended when I take advantage of them that way. I just won't ask."

Doomsayer: "This is a scary, unpredictable situation. If anything bad were to happen, I would not be able to handle it. I need to avoid putting myself at risk of anything dangerous."

Before we go any further, see if you can create your own list of personal negative self-talk themes based on what you've learned so far. Imagine yourself in a typical prospecting situation. Think about the mind chatter that might precede initiating contact with a client or buyer. Remember to use thought deceleration to help slow it down. Then write them down. If you get stuck, you can use the examples above, as well as the list of mindbenders. Refer back to the chapter on Call Reluctance types and review the self-checklists for the ones you struggle with. We suggest you select one or two types that cause you the most distress and concentrate on those themes first. You can tackle others later if necessary.

Don't worry if it's not all coming together for you

at this point. Remember: negative mind-chatter is wily. Its job is to sabotage your best, most motivated attempts to succeed. It does that spirit-crushing work with stealth and dedication, and it may have months or years of experience. You're just getting started. Keep tuning in, keep practicing, and stay vigilant.

Step Three: Defanging the Call Reluctance Beast

Now you know (or know how to discover, if you're not quite there yet) what Call Reluctance sounds like in your own head. The next step is to call out negative self-statements for the lies they are. You unwittingly allowed them to live in your head. You can expose them, evict them, and install something better in their place. Here's how.

We'll start with a brief exercise. Put yourself mentally in a typical prospecting situation. Phone in hand, about to dial. Standing outside a potential customer's office. Waiting in the wings to speak at a sales presentation or seminar. Make it as real in your mind as you can. Now recite the following statement out loud three times:

"I must make them like me or I am nothing."
"I must make them like me or I am nothing."
"I must make them like me or I am nothing."

Even if you don't believe it, pretend you do. Chances are you've told yourself something like it in a real prospecting situation, just not out loud and not on purpose. But this time really sell it to yourself. Then mentally follow through: Make the call, face the customer, greet your audience.

How do you feel? How did reciting that statement influence how you perceived the situation? Did it affect your feelings about the likely outcome of making the call?

Feelings are an important part of our survival instinct. They don't like being placed in situations that could result in annihilation and…

Wait. *Annihilation*? Who said anything about annihilation?

You did. That's how you emotionally interpret a situation when you say " . . . or I am nothing." Based on what you've told yourself, the only information your feelings have about the upcoming prospecting situation is:

- You're about to call on someone who is not expecting your call.
- You must make everybody like you.
- If anyone doesn't like or approve of you, you will cease to exist.
- Therefore, you're about to place yourself in a situation that threatens your very survival.

What fun.

This can't possibly be how you want to feel every time you prospect. So how do you change this scenario? By replacing your fear-producing self-statements with neutral or positive ones. To illustrate, let's return to our thought experiment. Imagine yourself in the exact same prospecting situation as before. But this time, recite the following amended version of the previous statement three times:

"It would be great if they like me, but I can only do my best."

"It would be great if they like me, but I can only do my best."

"It would be great if they like me, but I can only do my best."

Consider how you feel now as you imagine making the call. Notice the difference in the role your feelings play. In the first act, they were told a disaster might occur if you dialed the phone, etc. In the second act, you substituted a judgment-free preference, but not an ultimatum; there was no either-or, no doomsday alarm.

In short, the first version presents the threat of annihilation; the second presents an opportunity. Of the two, which statement is more true? Which is goal-supporting? Which takes more energy to act on? We hope the difference — and your choice — is clear.

Self-Supporting vs. Self-Limiting Mind Chatter: What's the Difference?

Successfully applying Thought Realignment requires you to identify negative mind chatter when it chimes in so that you can challenge it. But that's not always easy.

If you've spent a long time struggling with Call Reluctance, your emotional filters may be clogged from over-use. Years of trying to "fix" yourself with self-help books, positive affirmations, short-term attitude boosters and other mind tricks may have left you unable to tell the difference between what is actually helpful and what simply reinforces your hesitation and frustration.

A quick trip to the Internet provides a wealth of advice for would-be sales superstars. They include suggested affirmations as well as nuggets of wisdom for overcoming "the fear of rejection." They all, presumably, are well-meaning. But are they self-supporting or self-limiting? Here are some actual examples we've found online:

- I love my job every day that I work.
- All of my relationships are positive and filled with love and compassion.
- Overcome your fears by following your dreams.
- Fear of rejection is the one condition for which there is no cure, no little pill and no quick fix. The choice is yours, deal with it or get out of sales.
- If you don't truly believe you can achieve those big money goals you set each year, no action you ever take will create the long-term success you desire.
- There is nothing to fear if you just take the action steps needed. The universe will align the right things that you need to achieve your goals.
- Great sales teams are made up of people who love to help others, not money-hungry opportunists.

And our personal favorite positive affirmation:

- Today, I will not take advice from anyone who is more messed up than I am.

Sometimes slowed-down mind chatter is clearly negative, such as "If I can't answer every single question a prospect asks, I'll never make a sale, and then I'll be a complete failure." But what if, based on exposure to the above advice, you tell yourself "I don't fear anything because the universe will take care of me"? How can having the entire universe on your side be anything but self-supporting?

As you begin to re-align your thoughts and transform negative mind chatter into positive self-statements, it's important to remember two guiding principles:

1. Positive thoughts about something can't simply replace negative thoughts about the same thing. They're two separate entities. Your mind is capable of housing both and letting them grapple for control of your emotions.

2. Sometimes thoughts that seem positive are actually concealing negative (or at least unproductive) attitudes via hopeful-sounding words. This is especially true when they're coming from an outside source.

If you truly associate certain types of prospecting with feelings of anxiety, inferiority, and dread, then simply telling yourself "I love making phone calls!" or "Calling on doctors and lawyers is my favorite thing in the world!" is not going to magically snuff out those feelings. Nor are "positive" affirmations such as "I'm a professional adviser, not a money-grubbing peddler" going to erase a deep-seated (albeit inaccurate) fear that you may be that very thing. In fact, the cognitive dissonance that can result from continually telling yourself one thing while believing another can eventually lead to greater distress and even career burnout.

Don't play games with your mind. And don't let other people do it for you.

To help further discern the difference between self-supporting vs. self-limiting thoughts, we've put together this table of characteristics of both. Apply them to your personal mind chatter, as well as to the examples above or messages you've encountered in your own search for knowledge. Can you see through the feel-good haze and perceive the truth?

Self-Supporting Thoughts	Self-Limiting Thoughts
Offer flexibility in how you react to a given situation	Rigidly dictate how you must feel, even if the situation changes
Permit positive action against problems	Always present a self-defensive response
Help you feel in control	Take control of how you feel (you're just along for the ride)
Allow you to consider options	Insist that you have no other options (be on the alert for categorical language like "always," "never," "I must," "I can't")

Finally, here are a few examples to help you reprogram your Self-Propaganda Channel with more supportive messages. Try them, and then try to create your own.

Instead of: "If I make a single factual mistake on this call, I'll lose the sale, and that will be the end of my career."

Try: "Even if I'm not 100 percent sure of all the facts, I can still have a successful call based on what I know now."

Instead of: "If I have one more bad call, that's it, I'm not making another call for the rest of the day."

Try: "A negative reaction isn't the end of the world. If nothing else, I can learn from it and use it on the next call."

Instead of: "That company is full of snobs with advanced degrees. They're not going to listen to someone like me, so why bother trying?"

Try: "No matter how educated they are, they don't know my product the way I do. I can educate them."

Instead of: "Who do they think they are, judging me like a common salesperson? The next prospect who talks down to me is going to be sorry they did."

Try: "Other people's attitudes are not my problem. I'm going to be myself and do my best no matter what others say or do."

Instead of: "I can't make that call now. I'm way too upset."

Try: "Even though that prospect was rude to me, they're just one person. I can't please everyone, and I won't let them keep me from reaching my goals."

Now it's your turn. Take a few minutes to reprogram your Self-Propaganda Channel. What does your ideal prospecting playlist sound like?

Step Four: The Proof Is In the Prospecting

The problem with many attitude-shaping self-help programs is that they don't require you to *do* anything. Which raises the question: How do you know your attitude has changed if your behavior hasn't?

As a Call Reluctance countermeasure, Thought Realignment would fall woefully short of the mark if it only helped you know yourself better or feel better about yourself. Those are commendable goals, but they're better left to professional pep-talkers and their weekly feel-good podcasts. Insight is not our primary objective. Increased prospecting is.

In keeping with that aim, the next step in Thought Realignment is to translate what you've learned into more prospecting activity. Nothing more, nothing less. Do you hesitate to call on educated, professional people? Then your action objective is to initiate contact with more educated, professional people more often. Period. Do you allow yourself to sacrifice prospecting opportunities to persistent worry about low-probability catastrophes? It's time to challenge those worries, reclaim that energy, and channel it into making more calls.

The next time you begin to prospect, and those familiar self-sabotaging statements rear their ugly head, challenge their validity. Demand to know why and how unsupported, irrational thoughts should be able to keep you from the goals you've set for yourself. Call shenanigans on their verbal poison. Don't let them off the hook.

In practice, each time you replace a self-limiting statement with a self-supporting one, you're daring the call reluctant part of your brain to satisfy three demands. We call them the Three Clearing Questions.

To your fears, they sound like this:

1. Where's the *proof* that this *has* to be a frightening situation?

Remember, past experience, no matter how persuasive, isn't proof.

2. Do I *have* to respond to this situation with fear right now?

Believe it or not, you don't *have* to be afraid when you find yourself in a difficult prospecting situation, no matter how you've responded in the past. You can choose to make a deal with yourself: Just for the moment, put your fear in a box and stash it on a shelf. Then, after you've made your prospecting calls, feel free to retrieve the box and have the biggest, baddest fear meltdown ever. But for now, allow yourself to proceed without fear, even if that's a tough choice to make in the moment. Try it. We've rarely, if ever, heard from salespeople who made this deal and actually found anything in their "box" that was worth fussing over. Somehow, left to its own devices, fear has a way of slipping through the cracks and disappearing.

3. Am I *required* to feel *so much fear* that I can't make the call?

Who is setting that requirement? Can you go over their head, just this once? (Hint: It's you, and you can.)

Every time you successfully challenge your old, unproductive thoughts, the outcome should be the same: Instead of making excuses, you can choose to make the call.

Now you may be thinking: Wait a minute. Doesn't forging ahead and making prospecting calls, even if I still feel uncomfortable, just reinforce the old, automatic fear response?

No, it doesn't. When you use Thought Realignment, you actively convince yourself of the truth of the situation while you're prospecting. You do this by reminding yourself that there's no objective reason to be afraid and that you can be afraid and allow yourself to make calls anyway. Then you immediately put your best self-persuasive efforts to work by prospecting as if you weren't afraid.

THOUGHT REALIGNMENT

THREE CLEARING QUESTIONS

Challenge Your Mindbenders

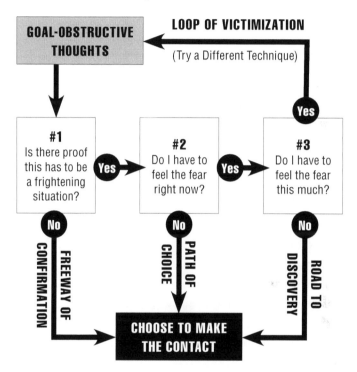

The combination of uncovering the source of your negative feelings and then practicing new, goal-supporting behaviors is what separates Thought Realignment from the "suck it up and make calls anyway" school of sales management. Forcing yourself to make calls without neutralizing underlying self-defeating beliefs invariably leads to mental and emotional anguish. How much "ketchup" can you convince yourself to ingest before the habanero sauce burns a hole in your stomach? As a coping strategy, it works for a few, but it kills careers as often as it cures. You may have tried it yourself. How did it work out for you?

To effectively reduce or eliminate Call Reluctance, remember this: supportive thoughts must precede productive actions, and productive actions must follow supportive thoughts. Having one without the other can be devastating to your career.

You Have a Choice

Should you always be gray-pinstriped rational in your approach to prospecting? We don't think so. It's not reasonable to expect your actions to be logical and self-supporting all the time. The objective of Thought Realignment is to help you discover (or recover) the ability to choose from among various behavioral alternatives, not to replace one form of self-limitation with another. We prefer having choices, even if they're not always rational. You should feel free to act mature or immature, caring or petty, optimistic or pessimistic, and even call reluctant when it so moves you. You deserve those choices. We don't want you to exchange one set of behavioral constraints for another, no matter what you read in a book. Even this book.

THE FINAL WORD

"Relentless, repetitive self talk is what changes our self-image."

— DENIS WAITLEY, Motivational Speaker

THOUGHT ZAPPING

Each day, the first time you see yourself in the mirror, you make a fundamental choice: Will I allow myself to be satisfied with what I see? Hopefully the answer most days is to acknowledge and accept what you see with a combination of grace, confidence, and a sense of humor. Unfortunately, for some doing daily battle with reflexive, negative habits, too often the choice is to ignore the objective image in the mirror and dwell on self-limiting barriers that are based on perception rather than reality. These conflicted souls trudge through their day, lugging those perceptions around with them like an overstuffed backpack, too preoccupied with the excess baggage to focus on their destination.

Some call reluctant salespeople are unable to prospect for the same reason. Their ability to thrive in sales is weighted down by the effort of coping with mindless, negative concerns about prospecting. In order to get through it, they have to force those feelings aside each time they approach certain prospecting situations. That takes effort. Effort takes energy. And energy used to *force* prospecting is energy not available *for* prospecting.

Is that you? If it is, then Thought Zapping may help.

Thought Zapping (Negative Thought Zapping, to be exact) is fast, effective, and easy to apply. Also known as "thought stopping," it's an adaptation of one of the oldest cognitive therapy techniques still commonly practiced by counselors and clinicians worldwide. It works by severing the link between negative thoughts that precede prospecting and the unpleasant feelings that accompany them.

With sledgehammer subtlety, Thought Zapping launches behavioral guided missiles to disrupt, disorient, and disengage undesirable thought-habit combinations. Once weakened, they can be replaced with more career-supporting attitudes about prospecting.

The Role of Habits

Habits play important supporting roles in our lives. They help make complex and repetitive acts possible — things like driving, walking, and various social interactions — without our having to constantly stop and think about them. Habits make our lives more enjoyable, and certainly more manageable, but some habits can make our lives miserable. Unpleasant, renegade habits of thought and feeling can conspire to create certain types of Call Reluctance. They're frustrating, perplexing, and annoying. They also keep us from earning what we're worth.

Fortunately, habits can be changed. But it's not always easy.

Every time you buy a new car (or rent or borrow one for a few days) you're faced with the challenge of changing old habits. Unless your new ride is the same make and model as your previous car, nothing is where it should be. You reach for the turn signal and the windshield wipers come on. You pull up to the wrong side of the gas pump because who thought it was a good idea to put it on *that* side of the car? And woe unto you if it's your first encounter with a push-button gear shift, you'll be reaching for that non-existent shifter until you don't know whether to curse or cry. Until you retrain your muscle memory and reprogram your thinking, the first few days usually are a comedy of errors, a transition so awkward it's funny. Almost. So every time you start to reach for the shifter, you stop and remind yourself, sometimes forcefully, that you need to press instead of pull. With time and repetition, you learn to approach the pump on the correct side. Eventually you develop a new set of habits for interacting with your four-wheeled baby.

This process can help alter all kinds of habits, including habits of thought and feeling. By repeatedly interrupting yourself whenever an unwanted emotional reaction asserts itself, and substituting — forcefully if necessary — a desired behavior in its place, an old habit dies and a new habit is born. That's how Thought Zapping works.

A Bad Habit's Worst Enemy

Negative thought habits associated with distressful feelings can be eliminated if they can be stopped in their destructive tracks. And they can, as the following exercise demonstrates.

You can try this with a regular clock radio or the alarm function on your phone. Tune the radio to a station you don't like, or select the most annoying alarm tone you can find on your phone. In either case, turn the volume up loud and set an alarm to go off in three minutes. Sit down in a comfortable, quiet place with the device nearby. Close your eyes. Allow yourself to think about the most fearful situation (not related to prospecting) that you can imagine. Being locked in a dark closet?

Singing karaoke? Whatever it is, really try to get into it, and stay with it until the alarm signals that your three minutes are up. Do this now, then keep reading.

So what happened? If you're like most people, several interesting things occurred. We ambiguously asked you to "think about" a fearful situation. How did you carry out the instructions? What did you actually do?

If you're like most people, you probably mentally conjured the situation first — the setting, the sights, sounds, other people or things involved. After that—a split second later, or several moments — you colored in the emotional landscape with fear, stress, anguish, etc. These occurred as separate steps that your mind then connected. Exactly how the brain accomplishes this multi-step process is an enigmatic scientific riddle that has captured the attention of some of the most gifted neuroscientists of our time. Understanding the mechanics isn't important here. What matters is that it does occur.

The relationship of this thought exercise to Call Reluctance is pretty straightforward. Every time you're faced with making a prospecting call, your brain scans your remembered experiences of prospecting to construct a memory of a past experience to guide your behavior. First the situation, then the emotions attached to it. If those emotions include fear, apprehension, or other negative reactions, you'll likely incorporate them into your evaluation of the current prospecting situation, as well.

The connection between what we recall and how we emotionally react to what we recall is essentially one of habit. The habit is continually strengthened, because each time we recall a particular event, we immediately summon the same feeling. Through repetition, the connection between the two becomes formidable until they're experienced as one. The bond is strong, but is it unbreakable? No.

To demonstrate, let's try a second round of the exercise you conducted earlier. Set another three-minute alarm. Sit down in a comfortable, quiet place. Close your eyes. Once again allow yourself to think about your most fearful situation, in as much detail as you can. Has anything changed?

Many people who try this experiment report that when they attempt to vividly imagine their fearful situation a second time, they're less successful. The memory of the sudden, loud alarm overshadows the experience. They can't help thinking about it as they repeat the exercise. It's almost as if the new, startling stimulus has driven a wedge between them and their fear.

So what's going on? What happened as you sat with your eyes closed, got into your disturbing event, and relived the distress that accompanied it? Three minutes passed, and the alarm went off. As it did, the bond uniting your memory to your feelings was momentarily interrupted. A new experience was introduced (hearing the alarm), which interfered with the previous connection between the situation you were remembering and the feeling you were experiencing. If you found it more difficult to re-experience your distress the second time, it means that after a single instance of having your attention shifted away from your feelings, your brain was already beginning to create a new association between your memory and your emotional reaction to it. That's Thought Zapping in action.

Weakening the connection between emotionally-charged thoughts and undesirable feelings can usually be accomplished within about five days. For highly motivated, goal-directed people, Thought Zapping can work within two days of conscientious use.

Listing your Negative Intruders

To begin, let's unpack your personal experience with contacting prospective buyers. What negative habits of thought and feeling interfere with your ability to prospect comfortably? On a spreadsheet or notepad, create a table consisting of two columns.

Title it "Inventory of Negative Intruders." Label the first column "Negative Thoughts" and the second column "Emotional/Physical Reactions." Keep this table with you for at least one work day, preferably two or three. Every time you prepare to prospect (or are in the process of prospecting), record *all* the negative thoughts and accompanying emotional reactions you experience. They should be easy to recognize, you've probably been lugging them around for a while. Don't try to evaluate or judge them, just write them down. These are your Negative Intruders.

Here's a sample inventory. Yours may include more entries or fewer, depending on how long and how well you listen to your self-chatter. (If you have trouble hearing or identifying your negative thoughts, try using Thought Deceleration as described on page 182.)

Inventory of Negative Intruders	
Negative Thoughts	**Emotional/Physical Reactions**
What if they ask me to give examples?	Muscle tension, heavy breathing
Oh no, I'm talking too much, aren't I?	Agitation, panic
This is my only shot — don't blow it.	Worry, dread
I can't handle another rude rejection today.	Hopelessness, heart races
If I offend them, I'll never make the sale.	Perspiration, distraction

Be honest and thorough in recording the things you worry about. These are the thoughts you must stop before they stop you. Worrying amounts to ineffective coping, which saps energy from your goals without returning a single ounce of profit or relief.

Tracking the Negative Intruders

The next step is important. Start it right after you've completed your inventory. Start a new table on your notepad or spreadsheet. This one is titled "Frequency of Intrusion: Pre." Set it up as shown at top on the next page.

Under the title, list any *one* of the intruding negative thoughts from your inventory. We recommend that you begin with one of the *least* distressing thoughts — one that may slow you down, but usually doesn't stop you. You can work your way up through your intruders in later sessions.

FREQUENCY OF INTRUSION: PRE	
My Negative Thought:	**Starting Date:**
	Measurement Period:
My Tally:	
TOTAL:	

Next, select a measurement period. The length will depend on your personal situation and goals. Do they require you to prospect daily? Weekly? How many contacts does it typically take to close a sale in your particular selling environment? Based on your circumstances, you may choose to track your negative intruder for a day, five days, or more. Remember: Be honest with yourself. Like all the countermeasures, Thought Zapping is effective only to the extent that you allow it to work.

Now you're ready to track the number of times your chosen negative thought comes to mind (intrudes) during the time period you selected. Be diligent. Record *every* instance with a hash mark, a check, whatever works for you. At the end of the measurement period, add them up and write down the total.

Here's what your completed Frequency of Intrusion table might look like.

FREQUENCY OF INTRUSION: PRE	
My Negative Thought: "I can't handle another rude rejection."	**Starting Date:** June 3, 2019 **Measurement Period:** June 3 – June 7
My Tally: XXXXXXX XXXXXX XXXXXXXXXXXXXXX XXXXXXXX XXXXXXXXXXXXX	
TOTAL: 51	

Zapping the Intruder

The goal of Thought Zapping is not to increase your self-awareness, but to change your prospecting behavior. Once you've documented how often a negative thought intrudes, it's time to do something about it. Get ready to zap your thoughts.

1. Place a rubber band around your non-dominant wrist. It should be large enough to allow circulation, and it should be thick enough to actually deliver a solid zap.

2. Sit in a comfortable chair and close your eyes.

3. Think about the intruder you selected. Remember a real-world situation that led you to record it on

your worksheet. Relive it to the best of your ability, including how it made you feel. When you begin to recall the negative reaction you experienced, do the following:

- Imagine the whole room (or sky, if you're outside) turning into a huge stop sign
- As you see the stop sign, imagine yourself shouting, "Stop it!" as loud as you can.
- At the same time, snap the rubber band against your wrist. Yes, it should sting. But once you begin this program, it's imperative to zap yourself every time you have the negative thought. Wherever you are. Whatever you're doing. (Note: Always zap yourself on the side of your wrist, or the top. Don't zap the bottom, where you might damage sensitive blood vessels just beneath the skin.)
- Immediately after snapping the rubber band, think of a positive mental picture of yourself. Recall a time when you did well in a similar situation. Recall a time you did well in a totally unrelated situation. Just remember a time and place where you felt good about yourself. Allow yourself to re-experience some of those good feelings. If you can't think of anything, then try to allow yourself to pretend.
- Now, while re-experiencing these pleasant sensations, mentally place yourself back into the negatively intrusive situation you are trying to defang. What happens? Most people have trouble focusing their attention on the

negative scenario. Every time they try, the
memory of the rubber band pops to their
attention. What about feelings? They start to
recall the revised, more positive feelings they
borrowed from a past positive event. A new
habit of thought and feeling is being born.

If you find any part of this process difficult, keep
trying. Focus on allowing yourself to substitute positive reactions for negative ones. Remember, you're not
trying to punish yourself for having negative thoughts.
That's not the purpose of zapping. You're simply trying
to remember what it's like to feel good when your first
instinct is to feel bad.

Now that you're familiar with Thought Zapping,
you'll find it's pretty easy to transfer to real-life situations.
Continue to wear your rubber band. Follow your regular
prospecting schedule. Every time your old negative thoughts
about prospecting try to intrude, zap your wrist and insert
your borrowed positive feelings. Monitor the number of
times the thought intrudes (see below). If all goes according
to plan, you'll notice a significant decline in the frequency
with which the negative thought intrudes. When it does try
to intrude, it will grow weaker with each zap.

You may have to actually use your rubber band only
during your treatment of the first negative intruder. After
two or three days of practice, it can be removed. Your
memory of the rubber band's effect will linger far after
you take it off, and from this point on, the phrase "Stop
it!" will have developed its own potency. We needed ours
longer than that. In fact, at times, we still use them today.

Measuring your progress

You can track your improvement by creating a "Frequency of Intrusion Table: Post," as shown below. Use it to track the frequency of your intruders once you begin Thought Zapping. It might look something like this:

FREQUENCY OF INTRUSION: POST	
My Negative Thought: "I can't handle another rude rejection."	**Starting Date:** June 10, 2019 **Measurement Period:** June 10 – June 14
My Tally (Pre): XXXXXXXX XXXXX XXXXXXXXXXXXXXXX XXXXXXXX XXXXXXXXXXXXX	**My Tally (Post):** XXXXX XXXX XXX XXXX XX
TOTAL: 51	**TOTAL: 20**

The difference you see between your Pre and Post numbers represents recovered motivation, energy that used to be dedicated to coping with prospecting, but is now available for making more calls.

What Thought Zapping Is — and Isn't

Superficially, Thought Zapping might appear to be just another form of positive thinking, with a gimmick attached. That's a reasonable inference, especially considering that it requires you to insert a positive thought at a certain point in the process. Nevertheless, it isn't.

Thought Zapping has little, if any, overlap with traditional positive thinking techniques.

Positive thinking and its various applications emphasize the value of positive mental imagery as a standalone cure for negative habits. They rely on sheer repetition to establish new habits of positive *thought*, assuming that the process will eventually lead to more positive *behavior*. Unfortunately, a clear link between positive mental images alone and measurable changes in productive behavior has yet to be demonstrated, except through anecdotal reports.

Positive thinking is essentially word-based. It relies on the use of verbal affirmations and often appeals to highly subjective concepts like the "unconscious mind" to explain otherwise unexplainable thoughts and behavior. Thought Zapping, on the other hand, is a mechanical procedure. It scrambles the automatic circuitry of undesirable, self-limiting habits, thereby decreasing the frequency of their occurrence. In our adaptation, the rubber band activates your inborn startle response to disrupt and disengage the linkage between an unpleasant memory about prospecting and the undesired feeling you've learned to associate with thoughts of prospecting. It zaps, if you will, your habitual response to a particular prospecting situation. Only after negative feelings have been interrupted can positive feelings gain any traction to help you change your behavior.

Thought Zapping is not aversion therapy, either. The snap of the rubber band doesn't serve the same purpose as electrical shocks applied to discourage negative habits like smoking and certain OCD behaviors. It's not done to *punish* negative thoughts and feelings, but to *disrupt* them and substitute more positive emotional responses. It's a crucial difference. If you can't allow yourself to accept the distinction (because of past experiences or self-harm issues), we recommend you try another one of the Call Reluctance countermeasures instead.

Spontaneous Recovery

Old habits die hard, and they don't always remain buried. Sometimes they resurface to haunt again, albeit to a lesser degree. The phenomenon is called spontaneous recovery ("recovery" in this case meaning the resurrection of the old habit). It's natural. You can expect it. If it happens, don't panic, and don't give up. Just have your Thought Zapper rubber band at the ready and give yourself a booster shot. After a few days of repeating the interruption-and-substitution process, you can get your prospecting goals back on track.

THE FINAL WORD

"I have learned that champions aren't just born; champions can be made when they embrace and commit to life-changing positive habits.

— LEWIS HOWES, American Athlete

SENSORY INJECTION

If you've ever lit a scented candle to "set the mood," cranked up the volume of a song that takes you back to your carefree high school days or hung a framed photo that reminds you of your best vacation ever, then you already innately understand the guiding principle behind Sensory Injection.

Our five senses — sight, sound, smell, taste, and touch — have a powerful impact on how we feel. They can trigger memories that make us happy, sad, angry, nostalgic, or festive. Those emotional reactions typically are automatic and instantaneous. We don't stop to analyze why the scent of Calvin Klein's Escape makes us feel 22 and in love again; it just does.

Connections between sensory input and the reactions they inspire can be strong, long-lasting, and indelible. They often form without our knowledge or consent. But what if, instead of simply experiencing those emotional connections passively, we could create them deliberately? We can.

The links between sensory input, memory, and behavior have been extensively studied. Market researchers, for example, have exploited them to influence buying behavior for decades. Large retail companies routinely pay hundreds of thousands of dollars to consultants who will craft a sensory experience that draws customers into stores, encourages them to stay longer, and influences what they buy and how much they spend. According to various studies:

- Customers spent 32 percent more money in a home decor store when the scent of citrus was wafted through the space.
- Visitors to a wine shop bought more expensive bottles of wine when classical music was piped in.
- Shoppers spent more time in a supermarket when music played softly in the background. Conversely, fast-casual restaurants frequently play music at higher volumes to encourage higher table turnover.
- On a company website, changing the call to action button (the one that encourages visitors to "Get Started" or "Sign Up Now") from green to red increased conversions (clicks) by 21 percent.

As a Call Reluctance countermeasure, Sensory Injection works on the same principle of influencing behavior, but in a proactive, goal-supporting way. By applying Sensory Injection, you can actually harness the power of your senses to reduce distressful feelings about prospecting and increase the number of contacts you're able to comfortably initiate.

In a nutshell, here's how it works. Many episodes of Call Reluctance are the direct result of learned reactions to external cues that you've identified as being emotionally threatening, like a telephone or a sales script. To the extent that your learned response to those cues is to feel fearful and anxious, you can't also simultaneously feel confident and hopeful. And if you've ever tried (and failed) to "pump yourself up" with positive affirmations, you know that those negative reactions can be visceral and tenacious. But with Sensory Injection, you can learn to forcefully insert more upbeat feelings into stressful situations by calling upon a secret weapon — a cue that is stronger and more positive than the Call Reluctance cue. Because this cue is delivered via one of the five senses, it can cut through distressful feelings in a way that self-administered pep talks can't. Unlike positive affirmations, which require you to believe them in order to be effective, Sensory Injection uses the physiological bond between your senses and your feelings to get the job done.

Sensory Injection is a collection of advanced attitude-shaping techniques. While they differ slightly in approach, they share the same objective: to push unwanted thoughts and feelings aside by attacking them at their base, where they are weakest.

Call Reluctance never occurs by accident. It's always a carefully orchestrated emotional response to outside stimuli you've learned to associate with distressful prospecting. For call reluctant salespeople, these have become reminders, or cues, capable of sparking Call Reluctance explosions. They do so now because they've done so before. What's more, each time they're permitted to trigger another Call Reluctance episode, they dramatically increase the odds that they'll do it again.

But the connection between Call Reluctance cues and emotional responses isn't permanently etched into memory. It can be tricked. That's where Sensory Injection comes into play. The external prompts that routinely activate distressful feelings when you prospect can be overridden by a sensory cue that you've chosen and trained to activate alternate feelings. Deploying this cue momentarily seizes your attention and steers it away from negative triggers, forcefully redirecting it to a substitute positive cue. Any sense can be used to create this diversion. You can experiment and decide which one works best for you.

All five of the Sensory Injection techniques follow the same basic sequence, differing only in the sense used (sight, touch, smell, taste, sound). We suggest you try working with your sense of smell first. Research shows that of all the senses, it has the strongest, most "pure" connection to the brain. That's why real estate agents deploy "homey" scents like fresh-baked bread and coffee during open houses, and why spas often smell like lavender or similar calming fragrances. The nose knows. Plus, olfactory Sensory Injection is portable, fun, and very easy to use.

NOTE: There are some important qualifiers. If your nose is chronically congested because of illness or allergies or if, due to some heinous trick of nature, your sense of smell is weak or missing altogether, scent-based Sensory Injection may not work well for you. In that case, experiment. Try a few of the other senses. One is likely to hit the mark.

With that in mind, let's begin.

Olfactory Sensory Injection Step-by-Step

We start with a choice. How would you like to feel when you prospect? More relaxed? More confident?

Keep in mind that these aren't opposite ends of the same scale. Relaxation and confidence are distinct feeling states. Becoming more relaxed doesn't automatically make you more confident, and vice versa. Can you work on both? Yes. But not simultaneously. The instructions for these two Sensory Injection applications are parallel, but not identical. There are important differences, which we'll explain as we go along. We've provided detailed, step-by-step instructions for creating both relaxation and confidence cues. Choose one to start with.

Relaxation

Despite how you may feel currently, prospecting isn't inherently unpleasant. It doesn't have to be stressful for you. The objective of this section is to teach you a practical technique you can use to depressurize your prospecting.

1. **Select a fragrance cue**

   Your fragrance cue is the stimulus you'll use to trigger a positive feeling state when Call Reluctance brings on feelings of fear and anxiety. It can be something you already identify with being loved, cared for, nurtured, contented, or relaxed. The smell of cedar or pine may remind you of relaxing vacations in a cabin in the woods. Or maybe the scent of your special Saturday night bath bomb gives you that warm and fuzzy feeling. If you can't think of a fragrance you currently associate with contentment or composure, then select one that's new to you that you can use to *create* that association. Whatever you choose, it should be something that you can easily carry with you. Essential oils in small bottles work well because they're portable and won't lose their potency over time.

Have some fun finding an appropriate cue. We've heard of people who have used everything from spent bullet casings to a special perfume to help them relax. What will you use?

2. Calibrate the desired emotional state

It's time to get calm. Think about what relaxes you the most. A certain kind of music? Yoga? Prayers? Going fishing? Meditation? Reading?

Relaxation is a highly individual matter. Use whatever works best for you. Feel free to use our Relaxation Procedure in Appendix B if you like. Audio recordings and free apps that can help you relax are readily available. On YouTube alone you can find guided meditation and a whole range of music and sounds that can serve this purpose. Find one that has the desired effect on you and adopt it as your own.

3. Connect the fragrance cue

With your fragrance cue close at hand, get calm and relaxed by your preferred method. Don't simply go through the motions; for Sensory Injection to be effective, it's important to achieve a state of authentic relaxation. If it's simply too difficult to do on your first attempt, don't force it; wait a few hours or a day and try again. Once you're in the relaxation zone, with as little physical motion as possible pick up your fragrance cue and breathe it in three times for about one second each time (if it's in a liquid form it may be easiest to put a drop on a cotton ball). Then put it aside and continue to relax for a few more minutes.

4. Fortify with practice

Repeat this sequence at least once a day for five days, allowing your fragrance cue to develop a strong association with the physical sensation of relaxation. Some people may require more than five sessions, some less. Use your own judgment, but we recommend a minimum of at least five.

When you've successfully completed your practice sessions, the hard part is over. Now comes the fun.

5. Aromashots: Stun gun for Call Reluctance

"Aromashots" is the name we give to the strategic application of your fragrance cue to help create a fear-free prospecting environment. Make sure you keep your cue close at hand: On your desk, in your car, in a purse or pocket, next to the phone, wherever you typically find yourself when Call Reluctance strikes. Then, *just before* you enter the habitually distressing situation, deploy (breathe in) your scent cue three times for about one second, just as you did during relaxation training in Step 3.

What's happening? Mentally, you might be issuing the familiar order to prepare for distress. But your specially prepared scent is delivering a stronger, clearer signal: relax. And if you followed the instructions carefully, that's exactly what your body will do. With your fragrance cue successfully deployed, and without the alarm bells of Call Reluctance distracting you, you can now refocus your energy on making the call.

6. Consolidate and reinforce

Now and then give your fragrance cue a booster shot. Renew the connection between your scent and the feeling of relaxation by repeating steps two and three a few times.

CAUTION: Never use your fragrance cue for any purpose other than combating call reluctance. Careless or inconsistent use can seriously weaken the ability of this method to achieve the results you desire. If your cue should ever inadvertently become associated with a negative event, abandon it and find something new.

Self-Confidence: The Feeling of Competence

Your sense of smell can do more than help you relax. It can also give you a boost of confidence to help optimize your prospecting performance.

Some self-help books improperly claim that if you purge yourself of negative feelings, you'll automatically feel positive. This book, if read too hastily, may seem to be guilty of the same claim. It's true that certain Call Reluctance countermeasures can help quell negative feelings that accompany prospecting. But they don't organically create a positive outlook. Dislodging a negative doesn't deposit a positive in its place. The two conditions are radically different. Just because you're no longer lying down doesn't mean you must be standing up. Used correctly, Sensory Injection can disrupt prospecting fear *and* subsequently trigger a feeling of confidence that can boost your productivity. Here's how.

1. Select a fragrance cue

   Follow the guidelines above. Remember to make it something portable.

2. Select a support person (optional)

   It's not absolutely essential that you work with another person. But it sure makes matters easier. Critical initial training steps are achieved much faster and require less effort. Having a partner also helps ensure that the technique will be as effective as possible. A trusted manager, trainer, colleague, friend, or significant other all make excellent support persons.

3. Select a Success Calibration Task

   Now you'll choose a task. It should be straightforward but challenging, something that takes you to the edge of your abilities, and then requires a little bit more. Choose a task that is difficult but accomplishable and that reflects skill and concentration, not just luck. Here are some examples:

   - Shooting free throws
   - Tossing beanbags aka Cornhole

- Throwing darts
- Pitching coins into a cup

Whichever task you choose, you must try to perform at a distance that is slightly beyond your current level of skill or native ability. Don't make it easy on yourself. Cheaping out now will all but ensure failure of the technique later, in the application step.

We recommend pitching coins for several good reasons. First, most people are unpracticed coin throwers, "amateurs" if you will, so they approach the activity without significant emotional noise. Second, it's logistically the simplest. It can be done in your office or home and requires only a cup like a coffee mug or a cookie tin — something that won't fall over easily, about 30 pennies, a reward cue (discussed next), and your fragrance cue. The instructions that follow presume you'll be attempting the coin toss but are basically the same for any task.

4. Select a reward cue

What represents achievement to you? Money? Recognition? Applause? Candy?

For this type of Sensory Injection to be most effective, achievement should be closely followed by reward, even if it's only symbolic. Choose something to reward yourself with each time you successfully pitch a coin into the cup. Your reward cue should be easily accessible, relatively plentiful, and something you value or desire. Small pieces of your favorite candy or dollar bills work nicely. In our workshops, we often conduct this exercise "live," with a volunteer tossing coins and the rest of the group cheering wildly (and sincerely) as a reward. (This can be a great team-building exercise and very effective if you can gather a supportive crowd!)

Whatever reward you choose, it must be given quickly and consistently, every time you get a coin in the cup and *only* when you deliberately pitch a coin into the cup. You don't get rewarded for throwing all your remaining coins at the ceiling in frustration, only to have some ricochet off the wall and fall into the cup. There's no reward for close calls, best personality, or most improvement, either. Those aren't substitutes for consistent daily prospecting, and they don't apply to the coin toss, either.

5. **Give your fragrance cue and your chosen rewards to your support person.** They'll be in charge of administering both.

6. **X marks the spot**

Mark the spot where you'll stand while you toss your coins. Ask your support person to place the cup at a distance that should enable you to make the shot with about 50 percent accuracy. Try to guess the correct distance, but don't verify it by actually pitching coins yet. Then have the support person move it about 10 percent farther away. Hitting the target at that distance will require self-control, persistence, resilience, concentration, patience, and practice (just like prospecting). You'll probably find hitting the mark difficult, frustrating, and infrequent. But when you do, it will be a genuine achievement, a cause for celebration.

Once your cup is in place, your support person should stand aside, at the ready with your reward and your fragrance cue.

7. Connect your fragrance cue

Standing at your mark, start pitching coins one at a time. Remember, just as in prospecting, almost doesn't count. Don't stretch so far forward that you lose your balance, try to find clever ways to cheat, reinterpret the instructions, or beat the system. That drains energy that could be put to better use. Be careful: If you're prone to search for loopholes or find an easy way out, your rewards will be fraudulent and unfairly earned. Each time you successfully land a coin in the cup, your support person should immediately present you with a single reward, closely followed by one or two short whiffs of your fragrance cue. Make sure you don't inadvertently get any on your lip or nose where the scent would linger.

8. Consolidate

Every time you successfully complete a toss/reward/fragrance sequence, augment your feelings of achievement with voice and body cues. To do that, amplify the sensations surrounding your accomplishments by verbally confirming aloud: "I did it! I feel great!" (This is where having an enthusiastic group of onlookers can help.) A heartfelt smile would be a nice touch too, if it's genuine.

9. Strengthen

Continue pitching coins until you've been through the reward sequence at least five times. Ten is better.

Some salespeople will complete this task in less than 15 minutes. Others will take longer. If two minutes pass without reward, move the cup 10 percent closer. If more than 5 rewards are earned in a row, move the cup 10 percent farther away.

10. Fortify

Practice this procedure once a day for five days, allowing your fragrance cue to become automatically linked to feelings you associate with achievement. Twice a day for five days is better. The more time you invest in fortifying your fragrance cue before taking it into the real world, the better your results will be.

11. Fire when ready!

Now the fun begins. Anxious? Doubtful? Uncertain? Apply your fragrance cue prior to prospecting situations where you need to feel like you can perform at your best. Watch what happens. Out of habit, you may still be aware of looking about for distress cues. But your body is receiving a dose of concentrated, unmistakable notification to expect optimum performance. Go for it!

12. Renew the cue

Aromashots can transform your lifeless attitude about prospecting into spirited, positive expectation. But you have to protect your fragrance cue carefully or you could develop a tolerance.

The best way to keep your fragrance cue fresh is to renew it often. While experiencing a rush of exhilaration from highly significant or unexpected successes, get out your fragrance cue and smell it while saying aloud: "I did it! I feel great!"

All versions of Sensory Injection work the same way. They seize your attention and then activate previously rehearsed, attitude-enhancing states before potential Call Reluctance triggers can signal the presence of a threat. Using trained sensory cues, you can direct yourself to feel any way you want: confident, sexy, admired, accomplished, or relaxed. The possibilities are limitless.

Each version of Sensory Injection follows the same basic instructional sequence, so we won't go into detail on every step for each one. Instead we'll briefly describe each, highlighting important differences when necessary. You can take it from there, making any other adaptations you might need.

Visual Sensory Injection

A good deal of research is available on the physical and psychological effects of visual stimulation. Here are a few examples of how the body and mind respond to what we see.

- Violent imagery is known to cause increases in heart rate and perspiration in viewers. Watching a film clip of a crying baby causes a similar reaction (even without accompanying audio).

- Visual input can trigger the body's "fight or flight" instinct and actually cause the hypothalamus to react against potential threats before the higher levels of the brain can identify the threat itself.

- Exposure to blue/green light triggers production of the hormone cortisol, which makes us feel awake and alert. This is why many people use light therapy to treat Seasonal Affective Disorder and certain sleep disorders.

- The psychology of color plays a large role in sales and marketing. The next time you watch TV, pay attention to the commercials, especially car ads. You'll notice that luxury cars are almost always shown in black, while sports cars are likely to be bold colors like red or yellow, and cars marketed to younger buyers tend to be quirkier colors like bright blue, green, or orange. The colors are chosen to evoke a certain feeling about the type of vehicle being sold.

Visual Sensory Injection takes advantage of our body's visceral, automatic reaction to visual stimuli. Specifically, it creates a positive response to a visual cue that you can then insert into stressful situations to shape your reaction and modify your behavior.

The instructions for visual Sensory Injection are the same as those for using your sense of smell. Only the cue is different. As an example, we'll explain what we call the Blue Dot Technique.

Step 1: Select the feeling state you wish to later reproduce on cue. For the Blue Dot, we suggest relaxation.

Step 2: Produce the desired feeling state with music, meditation, etc., as explained earlier.

Step 3: Pair the feeling of relaxation with a visual cue. We use small blue dots with an adhesive backing.

Why blue? A growing body of research supports and confirms the utility of lighter hues of blue or green as more effective for inducing pleasurable, relaxed mood states. You can also use a color that you already associate with those feelings, or buy a package of stickers in assorted colors to see which one best conveys relaxation to you.

Step 4: Repeat the relaxation process over several days to strengthen the association.

After sufficient practice, take your visual cue to work with you. When you need to relax prior to prospecting, place your visual cue in your line of vision. The rest is automatic.

You can attach your visual cue to your phone, briefcase, monitor, tablet, presentation notes, car dashboard — almost anywhere you can see it when you need it. Remember to keep your visual cue out of sight when you're not actively engaged in prospecting. If it's always visible, you risk developing a tolerance to it, thus reducing its effectiveness as a positive cue.

Visual Sensory Injection is effective, but its potency varies from person to person. Usually, when it fails, it's because of insufficient or inconsistent practice. Sometimes it's due to undiagnosed Call Reluctance impostors. But if you're sufficiently motivated and goal-focused, and you follow the instructions, it can help you learn to relax while prospecting.

Flavorful Sensory Injection

Are there certain tastes you associate with comfort, like your mom's sweet potato casserole or homemade chicken soup? Does eating Halloween candy bring to mind happy childhood memories?

It may be true that you are what you eat. But it's equally possible to feel what you taste. Taste influences mood. Your sense of taste can also help you form a new, more positive orientation to prospecting.

It's well established that the chemical composition of what you eat and drink can alter your mood. There is scientific evidence that foods high in Omega-3 fatty acids (salmon, sardines, etc.) are useful in promoting overall positive mood and support central nervous system function. Caffeine, carbohydrates, alcohol, even some artificial food colorings all interact with the brain to affect how we feel after we consume them.

The mental connection between what we taste and how we feel is another matter. What you eat doesn't just get gulped in, chewed up, and then routed down to your stomach to be chemically dissolved into nutritional categories. We *taste* what we eat. After speeding along electro-chemical pathways to the brain, sensory signals from taste provoke memories and associations that have been formed by prior experience. They allow us to classify what we taste as comforting, obnoxious, stimulating, or exciting. A 2011 study demonstrated that people who sipped a sweet, fruity drink were less judgmental of other people's behavior than those who drank something bitter, and that they were more likely to describe themselves favorably after eating a square of sweet chocolate.[3]

Sensory Injection can help you harness the power of your taste buds to overcome call reluctant feelings. Here's how.

Using Sensory Injection to forge positive feelings prior to prospecting is straightforward and easy. The step-by-step instructions parallel those outlined earlier for using your sense of smell. First, select the feeling state you want to reproduce on cue later. Then achieve that feeling state and pair it with your flavor cue in a series of practice sessions. After sufficient practice, take your taste buds prospecting. When you need to fortify yourself with your feeling state, put your taste cue in your mouth. The rest is automatic, courtesy of your nervous system and the effort you invested in practice.

You can pair your chosen feeling state with any taste

you wish. Potential flavor cues are abundant, limited only by your imagination and what you can safely put in your mouth. Portable, easy to eat examples include:

- Chocolate
- Chewing gum
- Mints
- Cinnamon candy
- Lemon drops
- Nuts
- Dried fruits

As with all Sensory Injection techniques, it's important to protect your chosen flavor cue. To avoid emotional contamination, it should be something novel, not something you taste every day.

A final note: An even more direct approach to employing this type of Sensory Injection is to find a taste sensation that provides a quick, flavorful *distraction* from negative thoughts and emotions. If you want to wrestle your mind's attention away from fear just long enough to let you make a call, try taking a bite of something with a strong, even overpowering flavor. This is actually a variation of Thought Zapping (see page 200) in a flavorful form. Try a sour dill pickle. A lemon. Bitter chocolate (80 percent cacao). Raw ginger root. A spoonful of extra-spicy horseradish. Or, if none of these does the trick, find something else to slap your taste buds. Use your imagination.

Sonic Sensory Injection

From the moment we wake up, the hearing ear is greeted by an uninterrupted symphony of sounds. They can be witless and incoherent or stimulating and arresting. Sounds can grab our attention or cause us to inwardly reflect. At day's end, sounds can help quiet the musings of our mind and lull us to sleep.

Physically, sound is just a wave-like mechanical vibration of air, an energy flux over a given area. In terms of human experience, sound is much more. If you've ever created a playlist (or a mixtape, if that's your jam) of songs

---

What emotional reaction, if any, do you have to common sounds like these? Go online and find audio-only clips for each.

- Train whistle
- Ocean waves
- Tornado siren
- Owls hooting
- Fireworks
- Cats purring

Bonus: Go to https://**www.birthdayjams.com**/ and enter any date: The day you graduated from high school, got married, started your first job, etc. It will link you to the song that was #1 on the U.S. music charts that day. Give it a listen. See if it takes you back. You can also enter dates that have significance for sad reasons, but prepare yourself for less-than-pleasant reactions.

specifically to create a certain mood (joy, excitement, self-pity), then you innately understand the power of sounds to influence emotions.

Reactions to different sounds vary from person to person. While some produce a nearly universal response, like fingernails on a blackboard. Others are deeply personal, like a song that was popular when you were dating your first love. Still others are situational. For example, the sound of a gunshot is likely to produce a very different reaction from a champion skeet shooter compared to a combat veteran with PTSD.

Using Sensory Injection, certain sounds can be transformed into auditory cues. The cue you select can then be used to arrest Call Reluctance.

The training procedure is similar to the techniques we've already discussed.

Select a feeling state

Sounds can evoke a myriad of emotional reactions, making this Sensory Injection technique particularly versatile. Want to feel relaxed when making calls? Confident? Assertive? Zen-like? Chances are there's a sound for that.

1. **Designate a sound cue**
   You can use sounds you produce yourself, like a hand clap or a whistle or that strange tongue-popping noise that none of your friends can do. Alternatively, you can play pre-recorded sounds: church bells, snippets of songs, cartoon sound effects, applause, wind

chimes, the victory fanfare from your favorite video game, etc. Ideally these sounds should be compatible with the feeling state you'd like to produce, i.e., the sad trombone sound ("womp womp") might not give you the confidence boost you'd like.

2. Produce the feeling state

Use one of the techniques previously discussed.

3. Pair them together

If you're using a recorded sound, having it readily available as a sound file on your phone's home screen or your computer desktop works best.

4. Practice

Practice two or three times per day, every day, for three to five days. It will take some more than five days, others less. Make certain the connection between your sound cue and feeling state is sturdy before trying to use it to counter Call Reluctance.

5. Apply

Deploy your sound cue to fortify your attitude whenever you need to, preferably right before anxiety-producing prospecting situations.

Break the Sound Barrier

Sound cues can startle, soothe, or mobilize. They may also be heard by others who haven't been exposed to the principles of Sensory Injection. As a precaution, you should explain what you're doing to the people closest to you at home and work. Or consider using earbuds.

The sound you choose for auditory Sensory Injection is a matter of taste, preference, and function. Make sure you consult with your imagination and your sense of humor, too, because working with sound cues can be fun.

Tactile Sensory Injection

Touch is the last of the five senses you can harness in service of Sensory Injection. Although described last, it's far from the least important.

Our skin doesn't just keep our insides in. Skin is a properly credentialed sense organ. A living antenna of sorts, it continuously feeds streams of sensory data to our brain, where they're processed into watchful intelligence about what's happening out in the world.

Touch and emotion operate closely together under a reciprocal agreement to share data. This arrangement is recognized intuitively, even when it is unknown to our intellect. Physical contact often has direct, intense emotional consequences. Imagine your reactions to the following:

- A threatening shove
- An angry poke
- A kiss on the cheek
- A baby's tiny hand grasping your finger
- A tap on the shoulder to get attention
- A pat on the back to signal praise

The same type of neurochemical receptors associated with the brain mechanisms that regulate emotions have been found at various other locations throughout the body. Neuroscientist Candace Pert[4] reported that neuropeptides, biochemical substances associated with these neurochemical receptor sites, formed a communications link between the brain, emotions, and our immune system. Not coincidental to our purpose, these emotion-related chemical receptors tend to be concentrated at the body's sites for touch. "Emotions are not just in the brain, they're in the body," says Pert. Massage therapy guru Clyde Ford[5] claims that when he touches the body "doorways to the mind open and images and memories enter conscious awareness." Thus, he reasons, "The neuropeptide system can be affected through touch, and emotions can be stored and recalled through (touching) the body." If true, the sense of touch can be used to manage behaviors like Call Reluctance.

Call Reluctance Applications

Like other forms of Sensory Injection, touch can be used to snatch attention from Call Reluctance fear cues. Alternatively, it can be used to trigger positive feeling states associated with optimum performance.

No pain, no gain

Who wants pain? Perhaps you do, if you want to overcome Call Reluctance but don't want to master any of the primary fear management techniques.

Job one for your nervous system is "detect and report pain." Nerve fibers detecting the presence of pain have absolute priority over everything else. Period.

Readers suffering from migraine, cluster, or vascular headaches, conditions far more disabling than Call Reluctance, already know that. Those conditions force attention onto themselves and away from everything else. They're painful, incapacitating, and have little redeeming value, except perhaps one: They illustrate a little-used Call Reluctance management technique. Self-generated physical discomfort can take your mind off your fears. No kidding. One pain can block another. Physical pain can block emotional pain. You can shake off your Call Reluctance fears by making your body protest.

Behavior modification pioneer Dr. Joseph Wolpe used one of Pavlov's principles, called external inhibition, when he applied electric shock to a patient's skin to demolish phobic anxieties. Fortunately, less drastic measures may be as effective. To distract yourself from prospecting fears, treat yourself to one of these uncomfortable distractions:

- Put a small pebble in your shoe
- Slightly over-tighten your belt
- Weigh down your wallet or purse
- Put sharp-edged keys in your pocket (Be careful!)

You don't have to inflict pain on yourself to overcome Call Reluctance. There are gentler, equally effective ways to use touch to apply Sensory Injection. You can follow the same sequence for the other four senses to engineer a feeling state of relaxation or confidence. Tactile cues to trigger that state might include the following:

- Squeeze your earlobe
- Lightly bite your lip or tongue
- Rub a smooth stone (like a "worry stone")
- Stroke a small piece of faux fur
- Hold a very tactile toy (modeling clay, Kooshi ball, beanbag animal, etc.)

Your tactile cue can be anything you can touch or hold. Keep it handy when distressful feelings about prospecting begin to intrude, and deploy it to get yourself back on track.

The five senses have the important job of monitoring and interpreting the world around us. If one of our senses is missing or deficient, the others step up to help fill in gaps in our perception. And their job doesn't stop at simply presenting us with the sights, sounds, smells, tastes, and tactile sensations of the world around us. Through complex interactions in the brain, our senses influence our thoughts and feelings about what we perceive. Sensory Injection allows us to tailor a positive emotional connection between a sensory cue and a desired behavior, in our case, prospecting. As scientists, we don't claim to fully understand the neurophysical processes that make Sensory Injection work. But we know it does. Give it a try. All you have to lose is your fear.

THE FINAL WORD

"The senses don't just make sense of life in bold or subtle acts of clarity, they tear reality apart into vibrant morsels and reassemble them into a meaningful pattern."

— DIANE ACKERMAN, *A Natural History of the Senses*

FINAL NOTES ON THE COUNTERMEASURES

With that, we've reached the jumping-off point in our journey. It's time to stop talking about barrier-busting sales and start making it a reality for you. We'd like to offer a few words of encouragement to take with you.

"How do you know the countermeasures work?" is a question we're asked all the time. The answer is, we study the results of applying them every chance we get, in real-world settings, with actual salespeople and sales organizations who have attended our workshops.

Our Workshop effectiveness studies speak to the legitimacy of the countermeasures when learned in a workshop setting. From our perspective and experience, that's where the most dramatic and sustained improvements (i.e., increased prospecting leading to increased sales) occur. On the other hand, people (like you) who simply read the book and apply the countermeasures on their own typically don't send us their pre/post data to demonstrate how they turned out. Our limited statistical data suggest that it may not work as well overall, but maybe the book on its own is more effective than we think. Feel free to let us know!

We believe there's another critical piece of the puzzle when it comes to successfully applying Call Reluctance countermeasures: outside support. We encourage everyone to share their goals and their barrier-busting intentions with one or more people, whether it's a colleague, a friend, a mentor, or a significant other. They can provide moral support and hold you accountable.

For our organizational clients, post-workshop success

is achieved through the sustained support and discipline of management. All workshops delivered by our staff include mandatory four-week follow-up group sessions. These are essentially accountability and support meetings, and they also help us track workshop effectiveness in real time. For example, we might recommend someone try a different countermeasure if the current one they're working on isn't having measurable results. We've also found that in a group setting, peers tend to be conscientious about keeping each other on task, calling each other out when they hear excuses. ("Thought Zapping isn't working for you, Bob, because you're not doing it!") The participants' manager hears all this play out over the four weeks. Then, once the formal follow-up procedure is over, it's up to the manager to continue providing support, either in a group setting or one-on-one. For some sales organization this requires a shift in attitude and/ or culture from the top down. We help them create a "total no-excuse prospecting culture." If you're reading this book on your own, finding a similar accountability partner could be the key to becoming a "total no-excuse prospecting salesperson" and a relentless seller.

At the end of the day, whether you attend a workshop or go it alone, YOU are the one who decides if YOU will apply the countermeasures according to the instructions on a consistent basis. It's your choice to make, all day, every day.

Do you want to start earning what you're worth?

6

The Future of
Call Reluctance Research

The sales profession is always evolving. New technologies to tap into individual and organizational potential develop at a rapid pace. Our understanding of the human mind continues to grow. And our commitment to be at the forefront of these emerging breakthroughs never wanes.

The renowned Call Reluctance research of George W. Dudley and Shannon L. Goodson began in the 1970s and forms the psychological and spiritual spine of this book. But while we stand on their shoulders, we've never been content to rest on their laurels. Even today we continue to build upon their foundational work and expand our horizons to exciting new possibilities in Call Reluctance research.

Here are just a few of the areas of study that may find their way into future Call Reluctance assessment and training:

- **The neurological basis of fear.** Advances in neuropsychology are helping us to better understand the physical structure of fear in the brain. How do we "learn" to be afraid? What role does memory play in forming unproductive habits? We hope the answers to these questions will help us develop new techniques that essentially rewire the brain when the fear response is triggered by situations that shouldn't be considered fearful.

- **Analogical Fear Replacement (AFR).** This approach is a "side door" to overcoming heavily resistant forms of Call Reluctance, such as Oppositional Reflex. AFR techniques work by focusing effort on overcoming a fear that is similar to, but unassociated, with Call Reluctance. In our own work with salespeople we often see that working on a diffused type (such as Yielder) can have a positive influence on a similar targeted type (such as Close Reluctance). We want to further study existing theories of psychological learning that have demonstrated how overcoming one fear can have a positive "ripple" effect on these adjacent fears.

- **Mindfulness.** Future research will also include a study of mindfulness techniques as they relate to reducing prospecting fears. While the term is sometimes minimized as simple meditation or a New Age trope, from a psychological perspective the concept of mindfulness is compatible with accepted techniques for reducing various types of anxiety. With its emphasis on mental focus and objectivity, practicing mindfulness is similar to some of the self-talk exercises common to mainstream cognitive therapy, which form the basis of Thought Realignment. We want to explore how it can best be applied to sales situations to help promote calmness and presence of mind and enable individuals to limit the intrusion of negative thoughts and feelings into prospecting situations.

- **Virtual reality programs.** Many Call Reluctance countermeasures rely on imagination or visualization exercises. Thus, their effectiveness is limited by the ability of the individual to effectively create scenarios in their head. Not everyone can do it well (the authors included!). A growing body of research suggests that some kinds of cognitive-behavioral therapy can be more effective when a computer-based "virtual reality" component is added. For example, the typical procedure for helping people overcome the fear of public speaking involves a series of sessions in which they gradually become comfortable with various situations, beginning with visualization exercises ("pretending" to be on stage) and gradually proceeding to staged "live" speeches and eventually an actual public speaking experience. When the early stages of the process are conducted in a virtual environment, the outcome depends less on the ability of the participant to imagine themselves in each scenario and gives the therapist more control over creating a realistic, supportive environment to reduce fear. Similar programs have been developed to help individuals with autism and ADHD to better manage social interactions. We're exploring the possibilities of this technology for Call Reluctance countermeasures to increase the odds of success in those not blessed with a naturally imaginative mind.

- **Mobile countermeasures.** Speaking of technology, we're always looking for better ways to administer techniques and training. One way could be the development of a mobile app to help salespeople apply Call Reluctance countermeasures. Acting as a kind of prospecting Fitbit, in the future an app might allow you to review techniques, set milestones, track progress, and send feedback to add to our database of real-world challenges and success stories.

- **New help for Yielders.** As the most common type of Call Reluctance, we want to augment our arsenal of knowledge to help salespeople manage or overcome Yielder tendencies. This may include refining existing techniques, developing entirely new countermeasures, and looking at established areas of study like assertion training to explore the best and fastest ways to yield results (no pun intended).

We're excited about the future of Call Reluctance research. But we know that the ultimate proving ground for our work isn't spreadsheets of data or controlled clinical settings. It's the real world, where prospecting, self-promotion, and advocacy produce real results.

When we say that initiating more contacts on a consistent daily basis puts hundreds or thousands of dollars in your pocket, it's not based on hopes, wishes, projections, computer models, or arbitrary targets. It's based on what people just like you have actually accomplished. Some of them started out with skepticism and even hostility toward our research. But when they allowed themselves to examine their fears, redirect their motivational energy, and transform coping into proud and purposeful selling, they began earning what they're worth. And so can you.

Our final word of advice: Don't just file this book among the others you've read. Admit that you could be doing more to bust through the barriers that have stood between you and your personal and professional objectives. Apply what you've learned. Be relentless. And discover (or rediscover) the joy of pursuing and achieving the success you deserve.

We welcome feedback from readers, workshop partic-ipants, and sales trainers. Please let us know if you have questions, comments, or ideas for future study. We'd love to hear from you! Visit us at www.barrierbustingsales.com.

APPENDIX A

WOMEN AND CALL RELUCTANCE

Call Reluctance and The Glass Ceiling: A New Perspective

Professional women: We have good news and bad news. The bad news is that it's 2019, and American women still haven't achieved wage equality. Despite gains, as of this writing women on average earn just 79 cents on the dollar compared to male counterparts. The good news (at least we think it's good news): the difference can't be attributed to Call Reluctance.

The wage gap, and the broader phenomenon known as the glass ceiling, have long been important ancillary topics to the work of our organization. Founding researcher Shannon Goodson began studying the glass ceiling and Call Reluctance in the 1990s. Back then, working women made about 72 cents for every dollar earned by men. Although the gap has narrowed, the Institute for Women's Policy Research estimates that, based on the rate of change, women may not receive equal pay until 2059. The authors of this book, being women ourselves, continue to be interested in dissecting and understanding the relationship between women's gains in the workplace (or lack thereof) and Call Reluctance.

Goodson's early research revealed that men had a slight edge in overall Call Reluctance scores. As a group they were less hesitant to promote themselves than women. At the time that seemed to fit with accepted archetypes (e.g., men have more confidence and ambition, women are more eager to please and "get along"). And it made sense as a potential contributor to well-documented disparities in earning potential — discomfort with self-advocacy leads to fewer opportunities for women.

But our most recent research paints a very different picture. Today, for all practical purposes the difference between men's and women's overall Call Reluctance scores is non-existent. Frankly, this came as a complete surprise to us. We had long taken the sex-based differences as a given. The obvious question was, Why? What changed over the course of 25 years?

We thought we were missing a critical variable, or looking at the data incorrectly. But after digging and analyzing and re-thinking (in true Over-Preparer fashion), we found . . . nothing. Nothing at all. The truth is, we don't know for sure why the Call Reluctance gap between the sexes has statistically vanished.

We have a couple of hypotheses. First, we believe that women themselves have evolved their views on the importance of prospecting and self-promotion. Encouraged by mentors and popular literature, they've invested time and effort into changing their behavior. Those changes have led to measurable (albeit not absolute) progress in the workplace.

Second, we've gotten better at measuring Call Reluctance. We developed a new Call Reluctance assessment tool (SPQ*GOLD/Full Spectrum Advocacy) that measures discomfort with prospecting much more accurately than previous tests. Now that we can interpret the data with greater precision, perhaps the difference between men and women was smaller than we thought all along.

Both of these factors are likely to explain the changes in Call Reluctance scores to some degree. But in the bigger picture, the gender pay gap and the glass ceiling are complex socioeconomic issues. We recognize that our Call Reluctance research may contribute to the conversation about why women earn less than men (and why some women succeed more than others), but can only ever hope to address a small subset of the factors involved.

Since Call Reluctance alone doesn't explain the difference in gender pay, we continue to look for other answers. One of the questions we ask ourselves is, "What do women want, and what are they willing to do (or sacrifice) to get it?" Why, for example, did we have fewer female than male applicants the last time we had an open sales manager position? We believe that pay and position inequality between men and women in the United States is a symptom of something. Obviously, the persistence of "boy's club" and "like hires like" mentalities plays a part. A single source or group can't be blamed, but wouldn't it be helpful if we could find a way that we women are contributing to the problem ourselves — and take control of it?

To the extent that we can take positive action to close the achievement gaps between the sexes, tackling Call Reluctance can play an important role in our success. Admitting that emotional hesitation to prospect and self-promote is limiting our earning potential, and learning to overcome it, are actions completely within our control.

In the final analysis, it doesn't really matter whether women are more call reluctant than men. Everybody has the same opportunity to reign in fear and kick it out of their way.

That's important, and empowering. Problems we cause are problems we can conquer. So women: Bust through your self-imposed barriers. Become your own best advocate.

Make yourself visible to decision-makers. Be relentless.

Men Vs. Women: Most Common Ways of Coping

Even though there is no statistical difference in overall Call Reluctance scores between the sexes (see above), our research shows that certain types of Call Reluctance are more prevalent in women than in men, and vice versa.

Over-Preparer is one of them. No big surprise there, as many current studies and surveys indicate that women still bear most of the responsibility for family management, including planning, scheduling, and budgeting, even when they have careers outside the home. Working women are chronically expected to know more, remember more, and deliver more as a result of that dual role.

Women also exhibit slightly higher levels of Yielder. This is likely due to lingering social mores that have traditionally equated assertiveness in females with being "forward" and "unladylike." The desire to avoid causing offense via such "inappropriate" behaviors is the calling card of Yielder Call Reluctance.

Among men, Oppositional Reflex is found more often than in women. In general, you're slightly more likely to encounter the behavioral characteristics of reflexive criticism and thin-skinned argumentation in the males of the species.

These behavioral tendencies represent real, verifiable differences between the sexes based on extensive Call Reluctance testing data. But before you start thinking that we (or you, or anybody) have uncovered the secret of "what working women are really like," take a long step back. That's not what we're saying at all.

First of all, remember — and we can never stress this enough — Call Reluctance types are not personality traits. They're learned patterns of behavior. Women may exhibit Over-Preparer tendencies at higher levels than men due to common past experiences, socialization, etc. But not all women do. And Over-Preparer Call Reluctance certainly isn't "caused" by being female. It's simply a coping mechanism that is slightly more prevalent in women than in men, for a variety of possible reasons.

Second, elevated Call Reluctance scores, whether Yielder in women or Oppositional Reflex in men, don't necessarily mean those behaviors are actively impeding their success. If overall Call Reluctance is low, then behavioral tendencies are just that: tendencies. Should an individual ever develop full-blown Call Reluctance, then knowing his or her specific predispositions is helpful to tackle prospecting discomfort and preventing future episodes. But in cases where a man and a woman are equally comfortable with visibility management, there's no evidence that sex-based differences result in disparities in income or opportunity.

Bottom line: Elevated levels of any Call Reluctance type can lead to energy being squandered on coping instead of prospecting. And that can be costly. But women are no more likely than men to suffer career-limiting consequences based on the shape of their fears. For better or for worse, Call Reluctance is an equal opportunity thief.

APPENDIX B

RELAXATION PROCEDURE

Some practitioners of relaxation techniques begin by relaxing a toe or a hand. They then move through every part of the body, step-by-step. The method described here is a short cut. We have learned from experience that for our limited purposes we can achieve the same results with much less effort and much less time. How? By teaching your brain a code word (SET) that prepares you to relax by first focusing your attention on relaxation. The word is not the process of relaxation itself. It merely signals you to focus your attention upon the process so that your relaxation response can then be easily triggered by the cue word (RELAX). Since you cannot relax and be tense at the same time, it logically follows that the relaxation response should spread throughout the body. When you find yourself in a potentially threatening situation, you can call up your relaxation response by saying your code word (SET) followed by your cue word (RELAX) and your body will re-experience the entire relaxation sequence. Try it!

To begin, find a quiet, non-distracting place and make yourself comfortable. You can either lie down or sit in a comfortable chair. You may wish to read the following relaxation dialogue into a voice recorder which you can play back whenever you want to practice this exercise.

Relaxation Dialogue

Begin by clenching your right fist tightly. Notice the other parts of your body as you feel the pressure in your right hand. Visualize your right hand clenched into a fist. Now, let yourself become momentarily aware of how you are breathing and how you can feel the tension growing in your hand and up your forearm as you see your clenched fist grow tighter. Now imagine that you are looking at your fist through a pair of binoculars. The binoculars have a special button on top of the lens near the front. Can you allow yourself to see it? Don't press it yet, but when you do it will flash a large, multicolored sign in front of your eyes that says, "SET."

As you feel your tightened right fist, take a deep breath and hold it for five seconds. Now, allow yourself to slowly exhale and press the imaginary button one time so you can see the word "SET," and as you do, slowly begin to relax your right hand. When it is relaxed, touch your left index finger to your left thumb and say to yourself, "RELAX." Pause for thirty seconds. Now clench your right hand again, take another deep breath, and hold it for five seconds. Exhale and press the imaginary button so you see the word "SET" again as you are slowly releasing the pressure from your right hand.

When your hand is relaxed, again touch your left index finger to your left thumb and say, "RELAX." Pause for another thirty seconds. Continue the sequence one more time: Clench, deep breath, hold for five seconds, press the button, see the word "SET," exhale, and continue to slowly release the pressure from your hand until it is totally limp. Then, again touch your left index finger to your left thumb and say, "RELAX." Now just pause. Don't do anything for five minutes except breathe deeply.

NOTES

1. Wiid, R., Grant, P. S., Mills, A. J., & Pitt, L. F. (2016). No joke: Understanding public sentiment toward selling and salespeople through cartoon analysis. *Marketing Theory*, 16, 171-193.
2. Bain & Company, 2013.
3. Eskine, K. J., Kacinik, N. A., & Prinz, J . J (2011). A bad taste in the mouth: Gustatory disgust influences moral judgment. *Psychological Science*, 22, 295–299.
4. Pert, C. (1999). *Molecules of emotion: the science behind mind-body medicine. New York: Simon & Schuster.*
5. Ford, C.W. (1992).Where healing waters meet: touching the mind and emotions through the body. Barrytown, NY: Station Hill Press.

INDEX

ABOUT THE AUTHORS

She's now the CEO of Behavioral Sciences Research Press, but **SUZANNE C. DUDLEY** literally grew up with the company. From an early age she worked on the "family farm" alongside acclaimed call reluctance researchers George W. Dudley and Shannon L. Goodson. Eventually striking out on her own, she earned Bachelor's and Master's degrees from the University of Texas at Dallas. After a successful career as a CPA she returned to BSRP in 2004 as Director of Finance, moving into the CEO role in 2018. Along the way she learned to conquer her own emotional barriers to success. Today Dudley's real-world business acumen and no-nonsense approach add an invaluable practical dimension to the data-based sales and management solutions for which BSRP is renowned. She enjoys sharing her struggles and breakthroughs with others and is grateful every day for the opportunity to help change the lives and careers of success-seeking professionals around the world.

TRELITHA R. BRYANT has a passion for helping organizations redefine success once they have identified and removed their barriers. As the Director of Research for Behavioral Sciences Research Press, she has completed hundreds of statistical studies on the influence of fear on the performance of salespeople and other professionals who rely on visibility management to achieve their goals. Her rock-solid research background allows her to provide needed clarity in the sometimes-hyperbolic galaxy of sales training and self-help programs. She offers credible insight into topics related to sales personnel selection, psychological assessments, and multi-national research. Bryant has a Bachelor's degree in Mathematics from Creighton University, has completed graduate coursework at Southern Methodist University, and has been a valuable part of the BSRP family since 1998.

Made in the USA
Coppell, TX
08 February 2022

73111691R10159